Spotlight Your Branding

CA Parinita Adukia

All Rights are Reserved
© 2025, CA Parinita Adukia

Table of Contents

Dedication

I dedicate this book to my parents Suresh Agarwal, Lalita Agarwal, my husband Harshit Adukia, my sister Palak Agarwal, my in-laws, my mentors, CA Anu Agarwal, CA Rajkumar Adukia, Sanjay Wadhwa, Sandeep Mukhi, my teachers and all my friends who have shown a constant support.

Also, thanks to my team at Portraiture, specially Rableen Kaur and CA Sakshi Ladia who helped me with the research and gathering the client data.

I would like to make a special mention, my daughter Manasvi Adukia, who inspires me every day to keep innovating and become better. Thank you.

Free Gift

Thanks for purchasing my book. I am grateful for your patronage.

Here is a free gift as a token of my appreciation for your buying my book.

> *You can book a free1 hour strategy call with me, where we can discuss your challenges and possible solutions to those. Let us get your branding sorted and get you clients.*

Also, because you purchased this book, you shall receive a discount of 20% on any of my services. Leave a mail on portraiturepari@gmail.com with your book copy and we shall generate a link for your purchase.

Acknowledgement

Why I wrote this book?

I have been a CA working in branding profession for 9 years. As a CA I have addressed and coached more than 25000 CA and CA students.

There is 1 common gap that I find is BRANDING.

Whether it because of the lack of inclusion of this aspect in the curriculum, or the structure of CA where it is about self-study, Ethical code or the traditional mindset of the community, CAs are not very open to the concept of marketing or branding themselves.

And this I feel is a major reason of missed opportunities by the whole community.

Hence, I felt it is of utmost importance that I share my experience and ideas around this topic with the fraternity and impact as many lives as possible.

Foreword

Dr. CA. Rajkumar Adukia

(Central council member ICAI, my mentor and Past Chairman WIRC)

I am delighted to introduce this remarkable book on personal branding for Chartered Accountants, authored by a visionary who has been at the forefront of this field. The author, a seasoned personal branding strategist, has transformed the professional journeys of countless Chartered Accountants. Her pioneering efforts have not only elevated individual profiles but have also shaped the broader narrative of branding within the CA profession.

Her contributions to the Institute of Chartered Accountants of India (ICAI) through impactful sessions, workshops, and thought leadership initiatives have been game-changing. By breaking down the intricacies of digital branding and seamlessly aligning them with the ethical principles of the profession, she has empowered CAs to establish themselves as thought leaders in their areas of expertise.

Beyond her association with ICAI, her influence has extended to various platforms where she has inspired both budding professionals and seasoned practitioners. Through her talks and engagements, she has demonstrated how branding can be a powerful tool to stand out, build meaningful connections, and achieve growth. Her insights, deeply rooted in practical experience, have made personal branding accessible and actionable for all.

What makes this book truly exceptional is the author's unwavering commitment to empowering the CA community. She doesn't just explain why personal branding matters; she provides a clear roadmap for how to achieve it. Packed with actionable strategies and innovative ideas, the book is a reflection of her passion for making a tangible difference in the lives of professionals. The testimonials from those she has guided speak volumes about the transformative impact of her work.

We CAs need a tremendous push and should definitely be working on our Branding as a community.

CA Manish Gadia
(Partner GMJ & Co, Past Chairman WIRC ICAI)

In an era where personal branding has become pivotal for professionals across industries, Chartered Accountants are uniquely positioned to leverage their expertise through a well-crafted personal brand. Yet, building a personal brand as a CA requires a delicate balance of professional ethics, technical knowledge, and strategic visibility — a task easier said than done.

It is with great pleasure that I introduce this insightful book on branding for Chartered Accountants, authored by a distinguished professional who has been a trailblazer in this field. The writer, a seasoned personal branding strategist, has not only demonstrated an exceptional ability to elevate the professional presence of countless Chartered Accountants but has also been instrumental in shaping the discourse around branding within the CA community.

Her contributions to the Institute of Chartered Accountants of India (ICAI) through impactful sessions, workshops, and thought leadership have been transformative. By simplifying the complexities of digital branding and aligning them with the ethical framework that defines our profession, she has empowered CAs to establish themselves as thought leaders in their respective niches.

Beyond her association with ICAI, the author's speaking engagements across various forums have further amplified her influence. From guiding young professionals to seasoned practitioners, her talks have inspired audiences to embrace the power of branding as a tool to differentiate, connect, and grow. Her insights, grounded in real-world experience, have made branding relatable and achievable for all.

What makes this book even more compelling is the author's relentless dedication to making a tangible difference in the CA community. She has helped professionals not only understand the 'why' of personal branding but also master the 'how' through actionable strategies and innovative approaches. The testimonials of those who have benefited from her guidance stand as a testament to the transformative impact of her work.

This book is more than a guide; it is a call to action for Chartered Accountants to step into the spotlight, tell their stories, and create meaningful connections. With the author's expertise and passion illuminating every page, I am confident that this book will serve as an invaluable resource for every CA seeking to build a brand that reflects their professional ethos and aspirations.

It is an honor to write this foreword and to invite you to embark on this journey of self-discovery and professional growth through the lens of branding.

Introduction to the Book

"The signature of a CA is more important than mine" Our hon'ble Prime Minister Narendra Modiji said this.

So good to listen to it right?

But fellow Chartered Accountants, our profession, as noble and essential as it is, comes with a set of challenges that can sometimes feel like an insurmountable mountain range looming before us.

Imagine this: You're diligent, hardworking, and incredibly skilled at what you do. But, there's a hitch. You're not sure how to market yourself effectively.

You're not alone in this struggle; many of us find ourselves in the same boat. When was the last time you scratched your head, wondering why those big firms seem to have it all figured out when it comes to attracting clients?

The truth is, they've mastered the art of branding that many of us are still trying to grasp.

But that's not the only hurdle we face. The ethical code issued by the Institute of Chartered Accountants of India (ICAI) restrains us from shouting our expertise from the rooftops. It's like trying to run a marathon with one leg tied to a chair. We are, in essence, the unsung heroes of the financial world, working tirelessly behind the scenes but often struggling to make our voices heard.

And then, there's the unrelenting competition. Big firms, with their deep pockets and extensive resources, cast a formidable shadow over us. It's like going head-to-head with Goliath armed only with a sling and a stone. It's tough, I get it.

As if that weren't enough, the markets we operate in are constantly shifting. What worked yesterday might not work tomorrow. Keeping up with these changes can feel like trying to catch the wind in a net. It's frustrating, to say the least.

And let's not forget the resource constraints. Unlike those big players, we often have limited budgets and manpower. We're expected to move mountains with a shovel and a wheelbarrow while they have bulldozers at their disposal.

So, dear colleagues, do these challenges resonate with you?

Have you ever felt overwhelmed by the ever-changing landscape of our profession?

Have you wished for a way to break free from the ethical constraints that limit our visibility?

Have you dreamt of a level playing field with Big 4's and other big firms?

Have you wished for more clients in your bag?

If you've nodded your head or felt a pang in your chest at any of these questions, then you're in the right place.

In the pages that follow, we're going to unravel the mysteries, address the pains, and chart a course to a brighter future. This book, " Spotlight Your Branding," is your compass, your guide, and your ally in this journey. Together, we'll navigate the treacherous waters of the CA profession, and emerge not just as survivors but as conquerors

Inside the pages of "Spotlight Your Branding," I'm going to unveil a roadmap that will lead you towards overcoming these challenges and thriving in your profession like never before.

In this book, I'm going to show you step by step how to revolutionize your approach to branding. We'll delve into branding strategies that will not only set you apart from the competition but also keep you well within the ethical boundaries outlined by the Institute of Chartered Accountants of India (ICAI). Yes, you heard that right – you can build a powerful brand while staying true to the principles of our profession.

First, we'll explore a range of branding strategies tailored specifically for Chartered Accountants. You'll discover how to showcase your expertise in a way that's compelling yet entirely ethical. We'll dive deep into the art of creating a brand that reflects your values, your expertise, and your unique selling proposition.

But that's just the beginning. We'll also explore offline marketing strategies that will help you connect with potential clients in a way that's personal and impactful. You'll learn how to craft your message and deliver it with confidence, whether you're in a room full of potential clients or addressing a small gathering of peers.

To complement your branding and marketing efforts, we'll also delve into the world of sales. I'll share with you the secrets of selling your services without feeling like you're selling your soul. We'll discuss how to build trust, handle objections, and close deals with finesse.

But we won't stop there. In today's digital age, leveraging the right tools can make all the difference. I'll guide you through the process of harnessing various digital tools and platforms to boost your visibility, connect with your audience, and streamline your operations. From mastering LinkedIn to using automation tools effectively, you'll have a full toolkit at your disposal.

And remember, all of this will be done ethically, within the code of ICAI. I'm here to show you that you can thrive in your profession without compromising your integrity.

So, get ready to embark on a transformative journey through the pages of this book. We'll equip you with the knowledge, strategies, and ethical compass you need to build a brand that not only grows your practice but also earns you the respect and admiration of your peers. The path to success begins here.

Now, you might be wondering, "Why should I place my trust in CA Parinita Adukia as my guide on this branding journey?" Well, let me paint a picture of the expertise and experience that I bring to the table.

I don't just talk the talk; I've walked the walk. As a Chartered Accountant myself, I intimately understand the ethical intricacies and constraints that we, as professionals, face every day. I've navigated the same waters, encountered the same challenges, and found a way to flourish within the bounds of ethical practice.

But my journey doesn't stop there. I've dedicated my career to helping my fellow CAs break free from the limitations that have held them back. I've conducted over a hundred sessions on branding, including prestigious appearances at the Institute of Chartered Accountants of India (ICAI). My mission has been, and always will be, to empower you with the knowledge and strategies you need to excel in a competitive landscape.

I'm not just an expert; I'm a faculty member at top management institutes, where I've had the privilege of shaping the minds of future business leaders. My passion for branding and my commitment to ethical practice have earned me a reputation as a trusted voice in the industry.

And when it comes to the digital world, I'm not just well-versed; I'm an authority. I've honed my skills to become a LinkedIn expert, helping professionals and firms amplify their online presence and forge meaningful connections. I've witnessed firsthand the transformative power of digital branding, and I'm here to share those insights with you.

I also run a podcast which features Chartered accountants, sharing their journey around their practice. (Link at the end of the book)

So, why should you trust me? Because I'm not just a branding expert; I'm a CA who understands your unique challenges. I'm a seasoned professional who has dedicated her life to helping others succeed. I'm a faculty member who imparts knowledge at the highest level.

I'm not just your guide; I'm your partner on this journey. Let's conquer the branding world together, the ethical way.

Now, let me paint a vivid picture of what awaits you when you embrace the strategies laid out in this book. Picture this: Mr. Anurag, an Internal Audit professional, just like you, who decided to take the plunge into the world of branding. He decided to harness the power of digital branding, and the results were astounding. He went from being a relatively unknown Internal Audit professional to a name that resonated in his industry.

In his own words, "I have experienced the power of digital branding as an Internal Audit professional. It has given me visibility and networking beyond my wildest dreams." Anurag's story is not an isolated incident; it's a testament to what can be achieved when you leverage the right strategies ethically and effectively.

Now, let's talk about the benefits you can expect to reap. Many CA's have applied the strategies discussed in this book and seen their practices grow exponentially. You'll not only witness a surge in the number of clients but also gain the visibility and credibility that you've been longing for. These strategies are not just some vague promises; they are tried-and-tested techniques that even the big players in the industry employ for their growth.

Imagine yourself in a position where clients seek you out, where your expertise is acknowledged and respected within the CA fraternity, and where you have the personal time and freedom to enjoy life outside of work. It's not a far-fetched dream; it's a promise.

We promise that if you follow the comprehensive guide laid out in this book, you'll experience a 3X increase in your clientele. You'll gain visibility and credibility that will set you apart from the crowd. You'll find it easier than ever to attract and retain clients, and you'll even find yourself in the same league as the Big 4 CA firms.

But, most importantly, we promise that you'll have twice as much personal time to spend with your friends and family, doing all the things you've been putting on hold. It's not just about growing your practice; it's about regaining control over your life.

So, if you've been waiting for a sign to take action, this is it. Anurag didn't wait, and now he's reaping the rewards.

Don't be the one who misses out on these opportunities.

Be the CA who seizes the moment, takes action immediately, and emerges as a true industry leader.

Now, let's dive into the heart of this transformational journey and unlock the secrets to building your brand and growing your practice. The time to begin is now.

Chapter1

In the heart of a bustling tier-two city in India, there lived a diligent and traditional Chartered Accountant named CA Meera. She was known for her unwavering dedication to her clients and her meticulous approach to her work. Meera had built a respectable practice over the years,

Meera often found herself buried under the weight of servicing her clients, leaving little time for growth or expansion. She watched enviously as big 4 firms effortlessly attracted high-paying clients and dominated the market. It seemed like an insurmountable challenge to compete with these giants. Meera knew she needed guidance, but she didn't know where to turn.

One day, she got an invitation to a special event by the Institute of Chartered Accountants of India (ICAI). She didn't know it yet, but this event would change her life. Then, someone important took the stage. It was CA Parinita Adukia, a friendly expert on branding.

"My dear fellow Chartered Accountants," Parinita began, "I understand the challenges many of you face in today's competitive market. As a practicing CA we are bound by the ethics, face tough competition from big firms and have limited knowledge on marketing and sales."

Parinita continued talking, and it felt like she knew exactly what Meera was going through. She talked about someone who was just like Meera, struggling to get better clients and facing tough competition from big firms. Meera couldn't believe it; it was like Parinita was telling her own story.

As Parinita spoke, Meera realized she wasn't alone in her struggles. Parinita said there was a way to make things better, a way to make her business stand out and attract better clients. It was all about how she presented herself, her brand.

Meera felt a rush of hope and excitement. She knew Parinita could help her, and she decided right then to learn from her. Meera knew her life was going to change because she was ready to learn how to make her brand shine and reach her full potential.

And so, the story of CA Meera began. With Parinita's guidance, she learned how to make her brand special and attract the right clients. Little did she know that her life was about to get much better, all because she decided to take the first step in making her brand stand out.

Brand positioning?

Brand positioning is a crucial marketing strategy that involves defining how a brand is perceived by its target audience in relation to its competitors. It's about creating a distinct and unique identity for a brand in the minds of consumers to differentiate it from others in the market. Brand positioning encompasses the key attributes, values, and associations that a brand wants to be associated with in the minds of its customers.

Branding is like your CA practice's special fingerprint. It's what makes you different from all the other CAs out there. Imagine it as your very own style, values, and the promises you make to your clients.

Imagine you're at a buffet. Each dish has its own place and purpose. Your brand positioning is like choosing the right dish that represents you best. It's about deciding how you want people to see you.

Personal branding is like creating a statue that looks just like you. You carve out your unique qualities, skills, and what you believe in. It's like creating a mini-you that represents your work.

Why Branding Matters for CAs

According to a statistic by ICAI, there are more than 90% CA firms operating as a sole-proprietor or a firm with less than 5 partners.

So why should you care about branding as a CA?

CA is a salesperson himself. A client will remember the CA and not the firm. That is the power of a CA. So, branding for a CA is very crucial as he is selling his service, through his brand, his name, his credibility. Branding helps him reach the right target faster.

You are the service provider, facing clients, hence clients will remember YOU.

Traditionally, we are focused on the numbers, the technicalities, and the paperwork. But in the entrepreneurial world, we're not just number-crunchers; we're visionaries. We understand that our brand is our secret weapon in a competitive market.

Entrepreneurial CAs leverage branding to build lasting relationships with clients. They go beyond the financial statements, offering insights, strategies, and peace of mind. They understand that their brand is the bridge between their expertise and their clients' financial goals. They go beyond the numbers, offering advice and peace of mind.

Here are some wise words to keep in mind:

*"Your brand is what people think of you when you're not around." - **Jeff Bezos***

*"In business, your reputation is your most important thing." - **Richard Branson***

Questions for Self-Reflection

Now, let's take a moment for some self-reflection. Answer these questions with a 'Yes' or 'No':

Do you have a clear idea of what makes you different from other Chartered Accountants in your field?

Have you thought about how you want clients to perceive you and your practice?

Have you identified your unique skills and values that can be part of your personal brand?

Do you believe that branding is essential for building trust with your clients?

Are you willing to go beyond the traditional CA role to offer more value and insights to your clients?

Have you considered the emotional connection your brand can create with clients?

Do you think of yourself as not just an accountant but as a financial advisor and problem solver?

Are you open to adopting a more entrepreneurial approach in your practice?

Do you see your brand as a tool to differentiate yourself and create lasting relationships?

Are you excited about the potential of branding to help your CA practice grow?

Interpreting Your Answers

Now, let's see what your answers reveal:

If you answered mostly 'Yes': Congratulations! You're already on the right track towards understanding and harnessing the power of branding for your CA practice.

If you answered mostly 'No': Don't worry; there's always room for growth. This chapter will help you start thinking about branding and its importance in your career.

Remember, building your brand and positioning yourself in the world of finance is an ongoing journey. Stay tuned for the next chapter, where we'll delve deeper into creating your brand identity. Until then, keep building your brand and growing your practice.

Strategy 1: Define Your Unique Branding Point (UBP)

Imagine your brand as a shining beacon in a sea of Chartered Accountants. To stand out, you must define your Unique Branding Point (UBP)Your UBP is the heart of your brand – it's what sets you apart from the crowd. Dive deep into your strengths, experiences, and passions. What makes you, as a CA, truly exceptional? Visualize this as your North Star, guiding you towards a brand that resonates with your clients.

What specific skills, experiences, or qualities do I possess that set me apart from other Chartered Accountants in my field?

How can I communicate my unique value proposition in a way that resonates with potential clients and makes them choose me over others?

Have I conducted market research to understand what clients in my niche value the most, and how can I align my UVP with their needs and preferences?

Strategy 2: Craft a Memorable Brand Story

Picture this: Your clients are sitting around a campfire, eagerly listening to your brand story. What would you tell them? A compelling brand story connects on a visceral level, making you relatable and memorable.

Why do CA's need a story? Remember we might not remember the face, the name or the work of the person, but we definitely remember the STORY…

Share your journey, the challenges you've overcome, and the victories you've achieved. Let your readers see your passion and dedication, and they'll be drawn to you like moths to a flame.

What personal experiences, challenges, or turning points in my career can I incorporate into my brand story to make it authentic and relatable?

How can I convey my passion for helping clients succeed through my brand story, and what emotions do I want it to evoke in my audience?

Have I considered the storytelling elements such as a compelling opening, relatable characters (including yourself), challenges faced, solutions provided, and a meaningful conclusion?

Strategy 3: Niche Down for Laser-Focused Impact

Visualize a magnifying glass concentrating the sun's rays into a single, powerful beam. Similarly, niche down your services to create a laser-focused impact.

Identify a specific industry or client segment that aligns with your expertise. By becoming the go-to CA in that niche, you'll establish yourself as an authoritative figure and attract clients who value your specialized knowledge.

What industries or client segments align best with my expertise, and which one am I genuinely passionate about serving?

How can I research and identify the specific needs, pain points, and challenges faced by clients in my chosen niche?

What steps can I take to position myself as an authority within my niche, such as attending niche-specific events, publishing niche-related content, or building strategic partnerships?

Strategy 4: Online Presence That Shines Bright

Imagine your online presence as a radiant showcase for your brand. It's imperative to have a professional website, active social media profiles, and engaging content. Your digital persona should exude trust, expertise, and approachability. When potential clients search for a CA, make sure they find you and are captivated by what they see.

Is my website user-friendly and visually appealing, and does it effectively communicate my brand's message and services?

What social media platforms are most relevant to my target audience, and how can I create and share content that engages and educates them?

Have I considered the importance of online reviews, testimonials, and client feedback in building trust and credibility for my brand?

Strategy 5: Cultivate Client Relationships

Visualize your clients not just as numbers but as relationships. Building strong, lasting connections with your clients is the cornerstone of effective branding. Be empathetic, attentive, and consistently deliver exceptional service. Happy clients become brand advocates, spreading the word about your expertise.

How can I enhance my communication and listening skills to better understand my clients' needs and expectations?

What personalized approaches can I implement to show clients that I value their business and are committed to their success?

Have I established a system for gathering feedback from clients and using it to continuously improve my services and strengthen client relationships?

These reflective questions will help you delve deeper into each strategy, assess your current approach, and develop actionable plans for implementing them effectively in your branding efforts.

In conclusion, the chapter "Positioning Your Branding" has taken you on a transformative journey, equipping you with essential strategies to elevate your brand as a Chartered

Accountant. As the World's Number 1 branding coach, I trust that you've embraced these strategies with enthusiasm and a clear vision for your brand's future.

You've learned the power of defining your Unique Value Proposition (UVP), which sets you apart in a crowded market, and crafting a memorable brand story that resonates deeply with your clients. Niche specialization has become your compass, guiding you towards laser-focused impact in an industry you're passionate about. Your online presence now shines brightly, attracting and engaging clients like never before. Most importantly, you've embraced the art of cultivating genuine client relationships, turning satisfied clients into your brand's most enthusiastic advocates.

As you reflect on these strategies and the reflective questions provided, remember that transformation takes time and effort. Embrace the journey, and be patient with yourself as you implement these strategies into your practice. Your brand is a living entity, one that will continually evolve and grow stronger as you refine your approach and deepen your connection with your clients.

With these tools in your arsenal, you're poised for success as a Chartered Accountant with a brand that not only resonates but also leaves a lasting impact. Your journey towards brand excellence has just begun, and the possibilities for growth and success are limitless.

Before we move ahead, the ICAI has laid down a set of Ethical codes which all practicing CAs must abide by.

The strategies that I have discussed in the book is out of my interpretation and experience with working with CAs and firms.

The link to the Advertisement guidelines is -

https://resource.cdn.icai.org/60968esb49621.pdf

Chapter 2

"Developing a niche isn't about limiting your opportunities; it's about amplifying your impact in a chosen arena."

The Pareto Principle, also known as the 80/20 rule, suggests that approximately 80% of a company's revenue comes from 20% of its customers. This underscores the importance of identifying and serving the needs of a specific customer segment or niche.

What is Niche?

Imagine this, a CA, dealing with direct taxation, having clients in Navy and is now popular in the Navy fraternity as the go to person for any tax related issue. They have many!!

That is Niche.

Imagine a CA, specialised in indirect taxation, having clients in diamond merchants, based in Surat. He is very popular as the best resource for any issue in GST for the community.

That is Niche

Niche is that special something that sets you apart from the crowd. It's what makes you an authority- A famous Chartered Accountant. But here's the catch: you need to know what that expertise is. You need to identify it, nurture it, and let it shine. Without it, you're just another number-cruncher in the sea of accountants.

Now, let's talk about niche. Your niche is your playground—it's where you thrive. It's that specific group of clients who not only need your expertise but appreciate it.

So, why does all of this matter?

We recorded a podcast with CA Manish Gadia, a reputed CA with over 27 years of experience. He extensively talks about why niche is important, how he developed it and how his it helped him.

He said "Thankfully very early in my career, I understood the relevance of focusing on one area of practice and I chose Indirect taxation."

Today he is a very re-known resource of GST, having delivered more than 500 sessions.

The podcast link is at the end of the book.

When you market yourself in a niche, you become the go-to Chartered Accountant for a particular group of clients.

You're not just a service provider; you're a-

Trusted advisor, a problem solver, and

someone who can truly make a difference in your clients' lives.

Imagine having clients who not only appreciate your work but also become your biggest advocates. Imagine having a practice that's not just financially rewarding but also deeply fulfilling. That's the power of expertise and niche.

In this chapter, we're going to explore the common mistakes that many Chartered Accountants make when it comes to expertise and niche.

Now when you meet a fellow CA or even when you introduce yourself, you have have generally heard "I am a CA practicing in all the areas"

What will be the takeaway of the listener, who is a non-CA?

Let us look at some of the mistakes on niche development you might be committing -

1)Lack of Clarity on Your Expertise

One of the biggest blunders you can make is not being clear about your expertise. Imagine going to a restaurant where the menu is a list all the dishes from different cuisines together, from Italian to Chinese to Mexican. You'd be confused, right? The same goes for your clients.

If you're not crystal clear about what you excel at, they'll be confused too.

Your clients want to know what you bring to the table, what makes you the right choice for them. But if your expertise is as clear as mud, they'll look elsewhere. So, the first mistake to avoid is the lack of clarity about your expertise.

2)Trying to Serve Too Broad of a Client Base

Think about it. If you're juggling clients from various industries with different needs and challenges, you'll spread yourself thin. You won't have the time or energy to truly understand and serve each client's unique requirements. This leads to subpar service and unhappy clients.

As a service provider, your time is your money. Hence smaller client base with focused results is your key.

3)Failing to Communicate Your Expertise Effectively

Even if you know your expertise inside out, it won't do you much good if you can't communicate it effectively. This is where many Chartered Accountants stumble. They use jargon and technical language that goes right over their clients' heads.

So, failing to communicate your expertise in a way that resonates with your clients is a big no-no.

4) Not Understanding the Evolving Needs of Your Niche Clients

Your niche clients are your bread and butter. They're the ones who value your expertise the most. But here's the catch—client needs evolve, industries change, and new challenges emerge.

If you're not keeping a finger on the pulse of your niche, you'll miss out on opportunities to serve them better.

So, there you have it—the common mistakes that many Chartered Accountants make when it comes to expertise and niche. But here's the good news: these mistakes are avoidable. In the next sections, we'll dive into the solutions you've been craving. We'll explore how to identify your unique expertise, choose the right niche, and communicate your value effectively. Are you excited? You should be! Your journey to expertise and niche success is just getting started.

Reflective Questions

- ✓ What areas of expertise do you believe you excel in as a Chartered Accountant?
- ✓ Are you currently serving a specific niche market, or is your client base too broad?
- ✓ How do you currently communicate your expertise to potential clients? What can you improve?
- ✓ Can you think of any examples where specializing in a niche could benefit your practice?

- ✓ Are you prepared to adapt to changing client demands within your chosen niche?

Developing your Niche

Now that we've delved into the common mistakes that practicing Chartered Accountants make when it comes to expertise and niche, it's time to turn our attention to the solutions they crave. If you're a practicing Chartered Accountant, this section is all about what you're looking for to supercharge your career and business. Let's break it down together.

Clear Identification of Your Unique Expertise

You want clarity. You want to pinpoint that one thing that sets you apart, that special knowledge or skill that makes you shine in the world of Chartered Accountancy. You're seeking a way to identify and articulate your unique expertise. After all, how can you communicate your value to potential clients if you're not even sure what that value is?

The solution lies in self-discovery. Take a step back and reflect on your journey as a Chartered Accountant -

✓ What do you excel at? What topics or tasks do you find yourself drawn to?

- ✓ What do clients or colleagues praise you for?
- ✓ What is the 80% of your income coming from?
- ✓ Do you have any unique certifications?
- ✓ Have you identified something that may have huge potential going forward and you are interested in it?

Sometimes, your expertise lies in the things you're naturally good at or passionate about. Once you've identified it, own it. Embrace it. This is your superpower, and it's time to let it shine.

Effective Strategies to Define and Target Your Niche Market

You want a roadmap. You want guidance on how to find and capture the right clients—the ones who not only need your expertise but appreciate it. This means narrowing down your focus, and that can be daunting. But fear not; there are strategies to help you find and define your niche.

Answer these questions-

- ✓ Who were your past clients.
- ✓ Who were the ones you enjoyed working with the most?

- ✓ What industries or sectors did they belong to?
- ✓ What specific challenges did you help them overcome?
- ✓ Which of these sectors can really grow in the next 5 years?
- ✓ What is the most unchartered territory for other CA's?

These clues can lead you to your niche. It's all about finding your tribe—the clients who resonate with your expertise and approach.

Once you've found your niche, craft your message to speak directly to them. Tailor your marketing efforts, your content, and your services to address their unique needs and pain points. This targeted approach not only attracts the right clients but also positions you as an expert in your chosen field.

Methods to Communicate Your Expertise to Potential Clients

You want to be heard. You want potential clients to understand the value you bring to the table. The challenge here is that many Chartered Accountants struggle with effectively communicating their expertise. It's not enough to know your stuff; you have to convey it in a way that resonates with your audience.

The solution? Storytelling. People love stories, and stories are a powerful way to communicate complex ideas. Share your journey, your successes, and even your failures. Explain how your expertise has made a difference in real-world situations. Use relatable examples to illustrate your points.

Additionally, leverage digital platforms. In today's digital age, having a strong online presence is essential. Maintain an active and professional LinkedIn profile, create valuable content, and engage with your target audience. Show them that you're not just a Chartered Accountant but a trusted advisor who can guide them through financial challenges.

Path to Becoming An Authority in Your Niche

Once you've identified your unique expertise, defined your niche, and mastered the art of effective communication, the next step is becoming an authority in your chosen field. This is where you step up your game and establish yourself as the go-to Chartered Accountant within your niche.

A bowler is not just a bowler in cricket, he will be a right-arm, fast paced, death over specialist. Right? Authority.

1)Establishing Authority and Credibility

You want to be the trusted expert. You want potential clients to see you as the authority in your niche, someone they can turn to for guidance and solutions. Building authority and credibility takes time, but it's a crucial step in growing your practice.

One powerful way to establish authority is through content creation. Start a blog or a YouTube channel where you share valuable insights, tips, and strategies related to your niche. Write articles or create videos that showcase your expertise. Don't hold back; the more you give, the more you'll be seen as an expert.

2)Continual Learning and Innovation

To maintain your authority, you must stay ahead of the curve. Embrace lifelong learning. Invest in your education and professional development. Stay up to date with industry trends and regulations.

Innovation is another key aspect. Look for ways to innovate within your niche. Can you develop new services or approaches that address emerging challenges? Adaptability and a willingness to evolve are qualities that set authoritative Chartered Accountants apart from the rest.

3)Building a Personal Brand

Your personal brand is how you're perceived in the professional world. It's not just about your expertise; it's also about your values, your style, and your reputation. Your brand should align with your niche and your target audience.

Take the time to define your personal brand. What do you want to be known for? How do you want people to describe you? Your personal brand should be reflected in everything you do—from your website and social media profiles to your interactions with clients.

4)Understanding Your Target Audience

To truly become an authority, you need to understand your target audience inside and out. You can't effectively serve their needs if you don't know what those needs are.

This is a very important step for your service.

The deeper you analyse your target audience, the better your solutions will be, and the content you provide them. Here's how to gain a deep understanding of your niche audience:

1. Client Persona Creation: Develop detailed client personas for your niche. These are fictional representations of your ideal clients, complete with demographics, goals, and preferences.

2. Pain Points – understanding the pain points and challenges will help you cater to better solutions and this will help you generate better results as well as satisfied customers. When you know the start

point well is when you get to your destination quickly.

3. Market Research: Conduct thorough market research to uncover trends, challenges, and emerging opportunities within your niche. Stay attuned to what's happening in your niche's world.

4. Feedback Loop: Actively seek feedback from your current clients within the niche. What do they value most about your services? What challenges are they facing? Use this feedback to refine your approach.

5. Regular Surveys: Periodically send out surveys or questionnaires to your niche audience. Ask about their evolving needs and how you can better serve them.

6. Competitor Analysis: Study your competitors who are also serving your niche. What are they doing well? What gaps can you fill? How can you differentiate yourself?

7. Personalized Solutions: Tailor your services and solutions to cater specifically to the needs and preferences

of your niche audience. Show them that you understand their unique challenges.

By understanding your target audience deeply, you'll be better equipped to address their pain points, provide solutions, and position yourself as the trusted expert they can rely on. Your authority will grow as your audience sees that you're genuinely dedicated to serving their needs.

Chapter 3: Get into Action

In the financial world, the mantra is often 'Act now, think later.' But what if I told you that this philosophy could be your ticket to a thriving CA practice? The key lies in understanding the power of taking action. It's not enough to be knowledgeable; you must be decisive, and sometimes, even a bit daring.

Your clients rely on you to guide them through the intricate maze of finance and taxation, and that's a responsibility not to be taken lightly. In this chapter, we'll explore how taking action can make you not only a better Chartered Accountant but a more successful one. It's time to step up your game, and it all starts with taking that first bold step.

One of the most prevalent mistakes is the dreaded 'analysis paralysis.' Your clients often find themselves drowning in a sea of data, unable to make a decision due to the fear of making the wrong one. They get stuck in an endless loop of research, weighing pros and cons, but rarely taking any action.

But, my dear CA friends, this is where you come in. You must help them understand that action, even if it leads to occasional missteps, is the path to growth. The world of finance is dynamic, and opportunities can slip through your fingers while you're busy overthinking.

Another common mistake is the resistance to change. Many clients are comfortable with the status quo, even if it means missing out on potential financial benefits. They fear the unknown and prefer to stick with what they know, even if it's not working optimally.

In this chapter, we'll explore strategies to help your clients overcome these challenges. It's not just about providing financial advice; it's about being a catalyst for change in their lives. It's about encouraging them to take calculated risks and venture into uncharted territories where financial growth awaits.

Reflective Questions

Challenge readers with thought-provoking questions:

- ✓ Are you currently stuck in analysis paralysis? How can you break free?

- ✓ What changes in your practice have you been avoiding? Why?
- ✓ Are your goals specific, measurable, achievable, relevant, and time-bound? If not, what needs to change?
- ✓ How do you currently manage your time, and what improvements can you make?
- ✓ Who can you be accountable to for your actions, and how can you track your progress effectively?

As we explore these key lessons, remember that these are not just random pieces of advice; they are the building blocks of your journey to becoming a world-class Chartered Accountant. Let's dive in!

Teaching Point 1: The Paralysis of Analysis

One of the most common pitfalls that Chartered Accountants often fall into is what we call "the paralysis of analysis." In simpler terms, it means getting stuck in a never-ending loop of thinking and analyzing without ever taking action.

As number and detailed oriented professionals, we tend to overthink, and ultimately, inaction.

The remedy? Understand that not every decision needs a mountain of analysis. Learn to make informed decisions swiftly. Set deadlines for making choices, and once you have the necessary information, trust your judgment and take action.

Teaching Point 2: Embrace Change

Change is a constant in the world of finance, especially in India. Tax laws, regulations, and economic conditions are perpetually evolving. To thrive as a Chartered Accountant, you must embrace change rather than resist it.

Indian businesses face unique challenges, and our ability to adapt and guide our clients through these changes sets us apart. Don't be afraid to step out of your comfort zone. Seek opportunities to upskill and stay updated with the latest developments in your field.

Teaching Point 3: Setting SMART Goals

Setting goals is crucial, but not all goals are created equal. In our context, goals must be SMART - Specific, Measurable, Achievable, Relevant, and Time-bound.

Specific: Define your goals clearly. Don't say, "I want to grow my practice," but rather, "I want to increase my client base by 20% in the next 12 months."

Measurable: Ensure you can track your progress. You should be able to measure your success in tangible terms.

Achievable: Set realistic goals. While it's great to aim high, be sure your goals are within reach with the right effort and resources.

Relevant: Your goals should align with your long-term vision and the needs of your clients in the Indian market.

Time-bound: Set deadlines for achieving your goals. This adds a sense of urgency and accountability.

Teaching Point 4: Time Management

Time is a precious commodity, and as Chartered Accountants in India, you often juggle numerous responsibilities. Effective time management is essential to maintain a healthy work-life balance and deliver quality service.

Start by prioritizing tasks based on their importance and deadlines. Utilize time management techniques such as the Pomodoro

Technique, where you work in focused intervals followed by short breaks. This can enhance productivity.

Additionally, delegate tasks whenever possible, and don't hesitate to leverage technology to streamline routine processes. This will free up your time for more strategic activities.

Teaching Point 5: Accountability and Tracking Progress

Accountability is a powerful motivator. It's not enough to set goals; you must also hold yourself accountable for achieving them. In the Indian context, where competition is fierce, accountability can make all the difference.

To implement this teaching point, establish an accountability system. This could involve sharing your goals with a trusted colleague or mentor who can check in on your progress regularly. Alternatively, you can use apps and tools to track your goals and measure your success.

Remember, accountability keeps you on track and ensures that you stay committed to taking action toward your goals.

In our Indian context, where the Chartered Accountant profession is highly respected, following these teaching points can elevate your practice to new heights. Embrace them as the foundation of your journey toward success.

As we proceed through this chapter, keep in mind that these teaching points are not just theoretical concepts; they are practical tools you can use to transform your practice and make a lasting impact on your clients and the Indian business landscape. Stay committed to your growth, take action, and watch your journey unfold with remarkable success.

The enemy of getting things done is "thinking"

So, stop thinking and get into action.

If you are avoiding meeting people, meet them NOW

If you have to call those leads, call them NOW

If you are thinking of getting on LinkedIn, sign up NOW

If you are thinking of that digital branding person, hire her NOW

<u>Hope you are making notes!!!</u>

Chapter 5:Ethical Code of ICAI

"**B**ut the Institute does not allow advertisements"

"Does the institute have any special clause around social media?"

"Are we even allowed to use CA as a prefix on social media?"

"Can we really use social media to get clients?"

These are some questions I regularly get asked.

Now, let's talk about something you're probably quite familiar with—the challenges you face due to the ethical code of ICAI. It's like having a rulebook that you must follow, and sometimes, those rules can be restrictive, right?

One of the biggest pains CAs feel is the inability to advertise or solicit clients. You might be thinking, "Well, how am I supposed to grow my practice then?" It's a valid concern, and we're here to explore solutions.

Imagine you have a fantastic service to offer, but you can't shout it from the rooftops. It's frustrating, isn't it? This is where the pain lies. You want to help people with your skills, but you can't always reach them easily.

What can you do to overcome these limitations while staying true to the ethical code? There's light at the end of the tunnel!

Firstly, it's crucial to understand that you don't have to abandon your dreams of growing your practice. You can do it, but you need to do it the right way — ethically.

Ethical marketing is your ticket to success. It's like the golden path that aligns perfectly with ICAI's ethical code. It's all about building your practice organically, without crossing any lines.

Fairly speaking the Institute has issued ethical codes around soliciting clients, directly and indirectly,

Clause 6- A member will be held guilty if -

Solicits clients or professional work, either directly or indirectly, by circular, advertisement, personal communication or by any other means.

This means, a CA cannot directly speak about his clients, ask for work, advertise himself, or put in public about his work.

Clause 7 –

A Chartered Accountant in practice shall be deemed to be guilty of professional misconduct,

if he: advertises his professional attainments or services, or uses any designation or

expressions other than chartered accountant on professional documents, visiting cards, letter

heads or sign boards, unless it be a degree of a university established by law in India or

This clause says, you cannot advertise your services on social media, or any platform, or talk about any other designations you have, other than CA and Dr.

There is some more explanation to these available on the ICAI website.

Even with these clauses, it does not mean he cannot market under ethics. There are ethical steps that a CA can take to brand themselves and in turn advertise their services.

We have also covered a very important podcast with CA Hrudyesh Panakhia, on the importance of values and following ethical codes, in practice.

(Link at the end of the book)

Reflect on these questions –

- ✓ What specific challenges have you faced in acquiring clients while adhering to ethical guidelines?
- ✓ How do you envision leveraging your expertise to attract clients through ethical marketing?
- ✓ Have you considered starting a blog or creating content to showcase your knowledge?
- ✓ What steps can you take to expand your professional network and generate referrals?
- ✓ How confident are you that your marketing efforts align with ICAI's ethical code?

Let us understand a very important concept for understanding the ethical codes and how to brand yourself - -

Inbound vs. Outbound Marketing for CAs:

Let's explore two marketing approaches — Inbound and Outbound marketing — and see how they relate to the ethical code.

Inbound marketing is like a magnet. It's about creating valuable content and building your reputation. You're not pushing your services onto people; you're attracting them by showcasing your expertise.

Now, outbound marketing, on the other hand, is more like a megaphone. It involves aggressive tactics like cold-calling or sending unsolicited emails. These strategies might lead to quick wins, but they can also violate ethical guidelines.

As a CA, inbound marketing is your best friend. It's about educating your potential clients, sharing your knowledge, and demonstrating your skills. This aligns perfectly with ICAI's ethical code, which emphasizes professionalism and integrity.

By adopting ethical inbound marketing, you can gradually build trust and credibility among your audience, ultimately leading to more clients.

Why Inbound Marketing is Ideal for CAs:

So, why is inbound marketing the ideal approach for Chartered Accountants? Here are a few reasons:

1. Alignment with Ethical Code: Inbound marketing is about providing value and building trust, which aligns perfectly with ICAI's ethical code. It allows you to market your services ethically.

2. Cost-Effective: While outbound marketing can be expensive, inbound marketing focuses on creating valuable content, which can be cost-effective in the long run.

3. Long-Term Relationship Building: Inbound marketing emphasizes building long-term relationships with clients, leading to loyalty and referrals.

4. Targeted Audience: With inbound marketing, you attract an audience genuinely interested in your services, increasing the chances of conversion.

5. Reputation Building: Through ethical inbound marketing, you can establish yourself as an authority in your field, which is invaluable for your practice's growth

Action steps for inbound marketing - For each points remember to refer to the guidelines of ICAI or consult a professional.

The book is built around these inbound, ethical steps the Chartered accountant can take to grow their practice.

Remember, the path to growth is open for you, and it's an ethical one. We've laid the foundation, but there's more to come in the following sections. Stay tuned as we dive deeper into ethical marketing strategies and ethical code compliance. Your success as a practicing CA is our priority!

In conclusion, as Chartered Accountants, your ethical code is your guiding star. Inbound marketing offers you a way to grow your practice while staying true to these ethical principles. It's about attracting clients organically by sharing your knowledge and expertise. So, embrace the power of ethical marketing and watch your practice flourish ethically and professionally. In the next section, we'll delve into specific teaching points to help you kickstart your inbound marketing journey. Stay tuned!

Here are some links to the ethical codes and FAQs by ICAI

https://resource.cdn.icai.org/73079faq58944.pdf

https://resource.cdn.icai.org/60255esb49076.pdf

https://www.icai.org/post/ethical-standards-board

Chapter 6:Online Presence

Having an online presence can increase your brand awareness by 80%.

First things first, let's talk about why online presence is crucial for you as practicing Chartered Accountants. In this section, we'll explore some eye-opening facts and figures that highlight the significance of being visible online.

Imagine you are a searching for a doctor to be treated from. What's the first thing you do? You guessed it – you Google it! And guess what? Your potential clients are doing the same thing.

Common Mistakes and Challenges you might be committing –

Now, let's address some common mistakes and challenges that many CAs face when it comes to their online presence. It's essential to be aware of these stumbling blocks so you can avoid them on your journey to building a robust online presence.

Mistake #1: Neglecting Your Online Presence:

One of the most significant blunders is neglecting your online presence altogether. Some CAs believe that their expertise alone will attract clients. While your expertise is undoubtedly valuable, it's equally important to showcase it online.

Mistake #2: Inconsistent Branding:

Another pitfall is inconsistent branding. Your website, social media profiles, and other online platforms should reflect a cohesive and professional image. Inconsistencies in your branding can confuse potential clients and erode trust.

Challenge #1: Limited Time:

I understand that you have a busy schedule. Balancing client meetings, paperwork, and deadlines can be overwhelming. Finding time to work on your online presence might seem impossible. But trust me, with the right strategies, you can make it work without burning yourself out.

Challenge #2: Technical Know-How

The digital world can be intimidating, especially if you're not tech-savvy. Setting up a website, optimizing it for search engines, or managing social media might feel like foreign concepts. But don't worry; you don't need to be a tech genius to succeed online.

Challenge #3: Content Creation

Creating engaging and relevant content is another challenge for many CAs. What do you post on your website or social media? How do you keep your audience interested? These questions can be daunting, but I'll show you how to overcome them.

The good news is that all of these challenges are entirely surmountable. It's all about having the right mindset and the right guidance, which is what this chapter is here for.

In the next sections, we'll dive deeper into these issues and explore practical solutions. We'll also take a look at a real-life success story that will inspire you to take action.

But before we move forward, I want you to take a moment to reflect on your own online presence.

- How strong is your current online presence?

- What specific challenges have you encountered while trying to establish it?

- Can you envision the benefits of an improved online presence for your practice?

- Are there particular online platforms you struggle with?

- Do you know which platforms are the best for you?

- Are you active digitally?

- How often do you get leads from online platforms?

Remember, we're in this together, and by the end of this chapter, you'll have a clear roadmap to enhance your online presence and boost your practice's growth. So, stay tuned for the next sections where we'll tackle these challenges head-on and start building the online presence you deserve.

Taking Action: Steps to Strengthen Your Online Presence in the Indian Context

Let's delve into the sixth section: Action Steps.

1. Audit Your Current Online Presence: Start by evaluating your existing online presence, which includes your website, LinkedIn profile, Google My Business listing, social media profiles, and even your WhatsApp business account. Assess the content, branding, and consistency across these platforms. Identify areas that need improvement.

2. Define Your Audience: In the diverse market, it's crucial to pinpoint your target audience. Are you primarily serving individuals, small businesses, or large corporations? What are their specific needs and pain points concerning the services you are providing? Tailor your online presence to address these audience segments effectively.

3. Optimize Your LinkedIn Profile: Ensure your LinkedIn profile is polished and professional. Update your profile picture, headline, cover picture and summary with your audience in mind. Use keywords that your clients might search for when seeking CA services. Be active on LinkedIn. Personally 80% of my clients are generated through LinkedIn. Use messaging and posting smartly.

(I take up LinkedIn course to help you generate more clients from it. Leave a mail on parinitaadukia@outlook.com to know more)

4. Leverage Google My Business (GMB): If you have a physical office or provide in-person services, create or optimize your Google My Business listing. It's vital for local visibility in India. Ensure your contact details, working hours, and reviews are up-to-date. The best part is, you appear in google search faster, if you are on GMB and your clients can leave reviews also, which will be totally ethical.

5. WhatsApp for Business: Utilize WhatsApp for Business to connect with clients and prospects. Share updates, answer queries, and provide a seamless communication channel for your Indian clientele. Ensure your WhatsApp business account reflects professionalism. Complete the profile section, with all your details, just like your website. Provide the links, your office address, cover photo (like your LinkedIn). It shows professionalism.

6. Content Calendar: Plan a content calendar with content relevant to the audience across platforms. This could include articles, posts, or videos on that are relevant for your audience which they may either find interesting or

informative. Consistency is key, so stick to your content schedule.

(If you wish to get a Content calendar as bonus, write to portraiturepari@gmail.com)

7. Engage with Insights: The biggest mistake you can make is just posting, because that won't take you anywhere. You need to be engaging with your audience regularly to show interest in their content as well. Your engagements should be insightful and share your expertise.

8. Encourage Audience Interaction: Actively engage with your audience on platforms like LinkedIn and WhatsApp. Respond promptly to comments on your posts and articles. Encourage discussions by asking questions and seeking opinions on topics relevant to India's financial landscape.

9. Collaborate with Professionals: Consider collaborations with other professionals, such as lawyers, business consultants, or industry experts. Collaborative posts or webinars can expand your reach and multiply your efforts to gain traction.

11. Publish Thoughtful Articles on Topics: Write and publish articles that offer practical solutions to Indian financial challenges. Address issues

like taxation, business finance, and investment within the Indian regulatory framework. Break down complex topics for your Indian audience.

https://resource.cdn.icai.org/60255esb49076.pdf

12. Engage in Business Forums: Join online forums, groups, or communities that focus on Indian business and finance. Contribute meaningfully to discussions, share your expertise, and connect with Indian professionals and potential clients.

13. Measure Your progress: Regularly assess the impact of your actions. Analyze your engagement, reach, and the growth of your Indian audience across various platforms. Use analytics tools to understand what content resonates best with your Indian followers.

14. Adapt and Evolve: The Indian financial landscape is dynamic. Stay flexible and adaptable in your approach. Adjust your online presence strategy as per the evolving Indian market trends and changing client needs.

Remember, building a strong online presence in the Indian context is an ongoing effort. Stay committed to your action steps, keep your Indian audience at the forefront of your strategy, and adapt to the ever-changing dynamics of the Indian business environment.

In the upcoming sections, we'll continue our journey to enhance your online presence within the Indian context. We'll explore more strategies and insights that will help you navigate the unique challenges and opportunities that come your way. So, stay tuned, and let's continue this exciting transformation of your online presence.

Chapter 7

Power of Social Media for Chartered Accountants in India

Introduction:

In today's fast-paced digital world, the influence of social media cannot be underestimated. It has evolved into a powerful tool for individuals and businesses to connect, engage, and grow. For practicing Chartered Accountants in India, embracing the potential of social media can be a game-changer. In this chapter, we will delve into the world of social media and explore how it can be harnessed effectively to propel your CA practice to new heights.

Mistakes and Challenges of the Customer:

Let's start by addressing some common mistakes and challenges that many Chartered Accountants face when it comes to using social media. Picture this: you create a profile on a social platform, post a few updates, and expect the magic to happen. But the reality is often far from that.

One prevalent mistake is the misconception that social media is a one-size-fits-all solution. Each platform has its own unique dynamics and audience. Using the same approach on Facebook, Instagram, LinkedIn, and Twitter may not yield the desired results. For example, LinkedIn is a professional network where you can showcase your expertise, whereas Instagram is more visual and informal.

Another challenge is maintaining a consistent online presence. Many CAs start strong but struggle to keep up with regular postings. In the digital realm, consistency is key to building trust and credibility among your audience.

Furthermore, some CAs are apprehensive about engaging with clients or prospects on social media. They fear negative comments or criticism. It's essential to recognize that social media is a two-way street. While there may be challenges, it also offers a unique opportunity to address concerns, provide value, and build lasting relationships.

Certainly, here are 10 reflective questions to help readers contemplate and apply the concepts discussed in the chapter on the "Power of Social Media" for Chartered Accountants in India:

1. Have you identified your specific target audience on social media, considering factors like their demographics, needs, and aspirations?

2. What are the most common challenges you face when using social media for your CA practice, and how can you address them effectively?

3. Can you recall a success story where a fellow Chartered Accountant used social media to achieve remarkable results? What lessons can you draw from their experience?

4. What are the key social media platforms that align with your target audience, and how will you tailor your content for each of them?

5. How can you leverage WhatsApp and Telegram for direct client engagement, and what types of content or updates would be most valuable to your clients through these platforms?

6. Have you considered starting a YouTube channel to share in-depth expertise in areas relevant to your practice? If so, what topics

would you cover, and how would you engage your audience effectively?

7. Are you actively participating in discussions and engaging with your audience on social media, or do you need to improve your engagement strategy?

8. How can you measure the effectiveness of your social media efforts? What key performance indicators (KPIs) will you use to track your progress?

9. Have you explored collaboration and networking opportunities within your industry or with complementary service providers on social media? How might these partnerships benefit your practice?

10. Are you staying up-to-date with the latest trends and algorithm changes on the social media platforms you use? How will you adapt your strategy to remain relevant in a dynamic digital landscape?

In the following sections of this chapter, we'll explore how you can identify your target audience effectively and choose the right social media platforms for your practice. We'll also discuss the power of WhatsApp and Telegram for client engagement, as well as the benefits of using YouTube and podcasts to establish yourself as a thought leader in the field of Chartered Accountancy. So, let's continue this journey into the world of social media and unlock its full potential for your CA practice in India.

Understanding Target Audience:

Now, let's delve deeper into understanding your target audience on social media. In the vast ocean of the internet, knowing who your ideal clients are can be your guiding star. For Chartered Accountants in India, identifying and connecting with the right audience can significantly boost your practice.

Firstly, consider this: are **you serving** primarily individual clients, startups, small businesses, or large corporations? Your audience can vary greatly depending on your niche. Knowing this helps you tailor your content and engagement strategies.

Secondly, think about the **demographics.**

 Are your potential clients young professionals, established business owners, or retirees? Understanding their age, gender, location, and income levels can shape your messaging and platform choices.

Thirdly, delve into their **pain points and aspirations**. What financial challenges are they facing? What are their goals? As a Chartered Accountant, your role is to provide solutions. By addressing their specific needs and desires, you become a valuable resource.

Lastly, assess which **platform** is your audience on? Are they active on LinkedIn, where professionals connect? Or do they spend more time on Facebook, a platform often used for personal connections? Different platforms cater to different demographics and interests.

Choosing the Right Social Media Platforms:

Now that you have a clearer picture of your target audience, it's time to select the right social media platforms to reach them effectively. In the world of social media, one size does not fit all, and each platform offers distinct advantages. You have to analyse –

- ✓ On which platforms are your audience one?
- ✓ What format of content works on which platform?
- ✓ What is the engagement level required on the platform and do you have time for the same?

Choose based on these questions. analyze

LinkedIn is a treasure trove for professionals. If you primarily serve businesses and professionals, this platform should be your go-to choice. You can showcase your expertise, connect with potential clients, and even join relevant groups to engage in discussions.

Facebook, on the other hand, is a versatile platform that can work for various target audiences. It's especially effective for local engagement. Consider creating a business page and joining local business groups to connect with potential clients in your area.

Instagram and **Pinterest** are highly visual platforms. If your services involve visuals, such as financial infographics or tax planning charts, these platforms can be powerful tools. Share visually appealing content to grab your audience's attention.

Twitter is known for its fast-paced and real-time nature. If you want to stay updated with industry trends and engage in quick, relevant conversations, Twitter is the place to be. It's also great for sharing bite-sized tips and insights.

Quora is one amazing platform. Here you answer queries and doubts which people post. Quora does require a lot of time and patience, but you are persistent can get you great results.

YouTube is the second-largest search engine globally and an excellent choice if you're comfortable with video content. Create informative videos about tax planning, financial advice, or industry news. This platform helps you establish yourself as an authority in the field.

Now, let's bring it back to the Indian context. India's social media landscape is unique, with platforms like WhatsApp and Telegram playing a significant role in daily communication. These platforms are fantastic for direct client engagement and personalized interactions. You can create broadcast lists and share valuable updates with your clients, strengthening your relationships.

As you navigate the Indian social media landscape, remember that regional languages can be a powerful tool. If your target audience predominantly speaks a particular language, consider creating content in that language to connect more deeply with them.

In conclusion, understanding your target audience and choosing the right social media platforms are pivotal steps in your social media journey as a Chartered Accountant in India. Tailor your approach based on who you want to reach and where they spend their online time. This strategic approach will maximize your impact and help you harness the full potential of social media for your CA practice. Stay tuned as we explore more aspects of the "Power of Social Media" in the following sections of this chapter.

Action Steps:

Welcome to the heart of our chapter on the "Power of Social Media" for Chartered Accountants in India. In this section, we will explore actionable steps that will empower you to harness the full potential of social media to grow your CA practice.

1. Create a Social Media Content Calendar:

- Start by planning your content in advance. A content calendar helps you stay organized and ensures a consistent online presence.

- Outline key dates, events, and topics relevant to your audience and industry.

- Consider using tools like Google Calendar or social media management platforms to schedule posts.

2. Set Up and Optimize Your Social Media Profiles:

- Begin by creating or optimizing your profiles on the chosen social media platforms.

- Use professional profile pictures and cover images.

- Craft compelling bio descriptions that highlight your expertise and services.

- Include contact information and website links for easy client engagement.

3. Identify and Create Valuable Content:

- Understand the needs and interests of your target audience.

- Create content that provides value, such as informative articles, videos, infographics, and tips.

- Address common pain points and offer practical solutions in your posts.

4. Engage with Your Audience:

- Social media is a two-way street. Engage with your audience by responding to comments and messages promptly.

- Join relevant groups and participate in discussions.

- Show appreciation for likes, shares, and mentions to foster a sense of community.

5. Leverage YouTube for In-Depth Expertise:

- If you're comfortable with video content, consider starting a YouTube channel.

- Create educational videos on topics like tax planning, financial literacy, or industry updates.

- Optimize your video titles, descriptions, and tags for searchability.

6. Harness WhatsApp and Telegram for Direct Client Engagement:

- Create broadcast lists to share important updates, tips, and news with your clients.

- Use WhatsApp and Telegram as platforms for direct, personalized communication.

- Share valuable resources, such as tax deadlines and financial insights, via these messaging apps.

7. Produce Consistent and Quality Content:

- Consistency is key to building a loyal following. Stick to your content calendar and maintain regular posting.

- Focus on delivering high-quality content that establishes your credibility and authority.

- Monitor engagement metrics to gauge the effectiveness of your content.

8. Collaborate and Network:

- Collaborate with fellow professionals, industry influencers, or complementary service providers.

- Networking can expand your reach and introduce you to new potential clients.

- Consider co-hosting webinars or guest appearances on each other's platforms.

9. Measure and Analyze Results:

- Use social media analytics tools to track the performance of your posts and campaigns.

- Pay attention to engagement rates, click-through rates, and follower growth.

- Adjust your strategy based on what works best for your audience.

10. Stay Updated with Trends and Algorithm Changes:

- Social media platforms continually evolve. Stay informed about algorithm changes and trends in your industry.

- Adapt your content and strategy accordingly to remain relevant.

11. Promote Client Success Stories:

- Showcase client success stories and testimonials. This builds trust and demonstrates the value you provide.

- Highlight how your services have positively impacted your clients' financial journeys.

14. Stay Ethical and Professional:

- Maintain a professional tone and ethical practices on social media.

- Be cautious about sharing sensitive financial information and ensure compliance with regulations.

15. Engage in Continuous Learning:

- Social media and digital marketing are constantly evolving. Dedicate time to continuous learning.

- Attend webinars, workshops, and courses to enhance your skills.

In the Indian context, remember to embrace regional languages if they align with your target audience. Using vernacular languages can create a more personal connection with your clients.

By following these action steps, you'll be well on your way to effectively using social media to grow your Chartered Accountancy practice in India. These steps are designed to empower you to connect with your target audience, build your brand, and ultimately achieve your business goals. Stay tuned for more valuable insights as we continue our exploration of the "Power of Social Media" in the upcoming sections of this chapter.

Chapter 8: Content Creation

"Content generates over 3x as many leads as outbound marketing and costs 62% less."

In today's digital age, where information is at our fingertips, it's crucial to harness the power of content to stand out in the crowd. You might wonder, why content? Well, my dear CAs, it's simple. Content is the key to building trust, credibility, and a thriving client base.

Why Content Matters for CAs in India:

As Chartered Accountants in India, you're dealing with a unique set of challenges and opportunities. The Indian financial landscape is constantly evolving, and your clients rely on you to navigate these changes. But here's the catch: they need to know you're not just keeping up but leading the way.

That's where content creation and sharing come into play. Through strategic content, you can showcase your expertise, build strong relationships with your clients, and establish yourself as a thought leader in the field. This chapter is your guide to making it happen.

Mistakes and Challenges of the Customer:

Now, let's talk about the hurdles many of you face when it comes to content creation and sharing. Don't worry; you're not alone in this. I've worked with countless CAs, and I've seen these challenges pop up time and time again:

1. Inadequate Content Strategy: One common mistake is diving into content creation without a clear strategy. You might be writing blogs or posting on social media, but are you doing it with a purpose? Without a strategy, your efforts can feel scattered, and you might not see the results you desire.

2. Lack of Time: You are busy professionals, and time is precious. Creating valuable content can be time-consuming, and finding a balance between your core work and content creation can be challenging.

3. Fear of Technology: Some of you might not be tech-savvy, and the digital world can be intimidating. The thought of setting up a website, managing social media, or starting a

YouTube channel might make you break out in a cold sweat.

4. Not Understanding the Target Audience: Effective content speaks directly to your audience's needs and concerns. If you don't truly understand your clients' pain points, you might miss the mark with your content, leading to disengagement.

5. Consistency: Being consistent in your content creation and sharing efforts is crucial. Many CAs start strong but then fizzle out. Consistency builds trust and keeps your audience engaged.

But fret not! The good news is, with the right guidance and a bit of practice, you can overcome these challenges and turn them into opportunities. This chapter is all about equipping you with the tools and knowledge to do just that.

I've seen CAs in India transform their practices by mastering content creation and sharing. It's not just about quantity; it's about quality and relevance. When done right, your content can be a game-changer, attracting the right clients and helping you grow in ways you never imagined.

So, my friends, get ready to dive into the world of content creation and sharing tailored for the Indian context. We'll address these challenges head-on and provide you with actionable solutions. It's time to take your practice to the next level and become the trusted expert your clients turn to. Let's get started!

Reflect on these questions -

1. What are my specific content creation goals, and how do they align with my professional growth as a Chartered Accountant in India?

2. Am I consistently producing content that resonates with my target audience and addresses their unique financial needs within the Indian context?

3. What are my specific challenges related to Content?

4. How effectively am I leveraging online platforms like blogs, articles, Quora, and social media to establish myself as a thought leader?

5. In what ways can I adapt and evolve my content strategy to stay in tune with the dynamic landscape, ensuring that my content remains relevant and valuable to my clients and audience?

Action Steps:

Now that we've discussed the challenges and solutions, it's time to dive into the action steps that will truly elevate your content creation and sharing game. Remember, the journey to becoming a content-savvy CA is an exciting one, and I'm here to guide you every step of the way.

1. Creating a Content Calendar:

The first crucial action step is to create a content calendar. This is your roadmap for what you'll publish and when. Start by identifying key dates and topics that align with your practice and your audience's needs. Think about the financial calendar in India - tax season, budget releases, and important regulatory changes. These are fantastic opportunities to create relevant, timely content.

Divide your content into different formats - blogs, videos, infographics, or podcasts - depending on what suits your style and resonates with your audience. Then, schedule these pieces throughout the year. Having a calendar in place ensures that you maintain consistency, a key factor in successful content marketing.

2. Identifying Niche Topics:

You're not just any Chartered Accountant; you're an expert in your field. Leverage that expertise by identifying niche topics that your clients are curious about. These topics should set you apart from the competition and demonstrate your in-depth knowledge.

For instance, if you specialize in taxation for startups, create content that delves deep into this subject. Explain complex tax codes in simple language, share case studies, and offer practical advice. By showcasing your expertise in niche areas, you position yourself as a go-to authority for specific financial matters.

3. Leveraging Blogs and Articles:

Blogs and articles are fantastic mediums for sharing your knowledge. Write informative pieces that provide value to your clients and potential clients. For instance, you can write about "Top Tax Saving Strategies for Indian Businesses" or "Understanding GST Updates for Small Enterprises."

Remember to keep these articles in a conversational tone. Avoid jargon as much as possible and provide actionable advice. Use real-life examples to illustrate your points.

Don't forget to optimize your articles for search engines to ensure they reach a wider audience.

4. Establishing Yourself as a Thought Leader on Quora:

Quora is a goldmine for showcasing your expertise. It's a platform where people ask questions, and you can answer them. But don't just give standard responses. Dive deep into your responses, offering comprehensive answers that demonstrate your knowledge.

Imagine someone asks, "What are the tax implications for NRIs investing in India?" Instead of a brief response, craft a detailed answer that covers all aspects of NRI taxation. Quora users will notice your expertise, and this can lead to inquiries and referrals.

5. Crafting a Strong Social Media Presence:

In today's digital world, social media is a powerful tool for content distribution. Choose platforms that align with your target audience. LinkedIn, for example, is excellent for professionals, while Instagram can work for visual content like infographics.

Share your content on these platforms, but don't just stop there. Engage with your audience by responding to comments and messages. Share relevant industry news and updates. Host live Q&A sessions to address common financial queries. Building a strong online community around your brand is invaluable.

6. Going Beyond Sharing: Engaging with audience

Remember, content creation and sharing are not just about broadcasting your expertise; it's also about engaging with your audience. Encourage discussions in your comments section or on platforms like LinkedIn and Quora. Pose thought-provoking questions or ask for your audience's opinions on financial trends.

Engagement fosters trust and builds a loyal following. It shows that you're not just interested in talking about your expertise; you're genuinely interested in helping and educating your audience.

7. Monitoring and Adjusting:

The content landscape is ever-evolving. It's crucial to keep a close eye on what's working and what isn't. Use analytics tools to track the performance of your content. Which articles are getting the most views? Which social media posts have the highest engagement?

Based on this data, adjust your content strategy. If you notice that certain topics resonate more with your audience, create more content around those themes. If a particular social media platform is driving more traffic, focus your efforts there. Flexibility is key to staying relevant in the digital realm.

Conclusion:

These action steps will set you on the path to becoming a content-savvy Chartered Accountant in India. Remember, it's not just about creating content; it's about creating meaningful, relevant content that positions you as an expert and builds trust with your audience. Stay tuned for more insights in the upcoming sections. Your journey to becoming a trusted thought leader in the Indian financial sector is well underway!

Chapter 9

The Power of Webinars for Chartered Accountants

As a CA we attend numerous webinars, be it through ICAI, study circle meets, or any business forums. But how to actually leverage webinars to get your branding done, let us figure out.

Why Webinars?

Benefits of Webinars for Practicing Chartered Accountants (CAs):

Webinars are more than just online seminars; they are a powerful tool that can take your career to the next level. As Chartered Accountants, you may wonder how webinars can specifically benefit you. Let's break it down:

1. Global Reach with Minimal Costs: One of the most significant advantages of webinars is their reach. You can connect with a global audience without the need for a physical venue or extensive travel. This is especially important for

CAs as your expertise can benefit businesses around the world. Think about the potential clients you can attract from different corners of the globe!

2. Establish Authority and Expertise: Webinars provide a platform for you to showcase your knowledge and establish yourself as an expert in your field. When potential clients see you confidently discussing complex financial matters, they're more likely to trust you with their financial needs. Your credibility soars, making it easier to attract and retain clients.

3. Cost-Effective Marketing: Traditional marketing methods can be expensive, especially for solo practitioners. Webinars offer a cost-effective way to market your services. With a well-executed webinar, you can attract a significant number of leads without breaking the bank on advertising.

4. Interactive Learning: Webinars allow for real-time interaction with your audience. This means you can address questions and concerns as they arise, creating a more engaging and informative experience for participants. In our line of work, where details matter, this direct engagement is invaluable.

5. Time Efficiency: As busy CAs, time is of the essence. Webinars allow you to share your expertise efficiently. You can cover important topics in a concise yet comprehensive manner, saving you and your audience time.

7. Lead Generation: Webinars are excellent tools for generating leads. Participants who attend your webinar are likely interested in your services. By capturing their contact information, you can follow up with tailored offers and convert them into clients.

8. Networking: In our profession, networking is vital. Webinars provide an ideal platform to connect with peers, potential partners, and clients. You can collaborate with other experts in your niche and build a network that can open doors to new opportunities.

Now, imagine harnessing these benefits to grow your practice. Webinars are not just a trend; they are a strategic tool that can set you apart in the competitive field of Chartered Accountancy. With your expertise and the power of webinars, there's no limit to what you can achieve.

In the chapters to come, we'll delve deeper into the world of webinars. We'll explore the common mistakes to avoid, tackle the unique challenges you may face, and provide you with actionable steps to become a webinar pro.

Certainly, let's rephrase the common mistakes made by participants while attending webinars:

1. Unpreparedness: It's a common blunder to join a webinar without adequate preparation. Participants should review the agenda and any pre-webinar materials to make the most of the session.

2. Neglecting Technical Details: Overlooking technical aspects can lead to disruptions during a webinar. Ensure your computer, internet connection, and required software are ready before joining to avoid unexpected glitches.

3. Multitasking: Engaging in other tasks while attending a webinar can reduce focus and comprehension. Treating webinars with the same attention as in-person seminars is essential to maximize the learning experience.

- Failure to Ask Questions: Many participants shy away from asking questions during a webinar. However, not seeking clarification or additional information can hinder your understanding. Don't hesitate to voice your queries, as others may have the same ones.

- Lack of Engagement: Webinars should be interactive. Failing to engage with your audience by not answering questions or neglecting polls and surveys can make your webinar feel like a one-sided lecture. Encourage participation to keep the audience engaged.
- Lack of Post-Webinar Action: After attending a webinar, not applying the acquired knowledge or neglecting to follow up with the host and fellow participants can limit the impact of the learning experience. It's crucial to have a plan for implementing newfound insights and fostering discussions or collaborations.

Certainly, here are five reflective questions related to the chapter on the "Power of Webinars" for practicing Chartered Accountants:

1. How can I tailor the knowledge gained from this chapter to my specific niche within Chartered Accountancy to maximize its impact on my practice?

2. What common mistakes mentioned in the chapter have I personally encountered or observed in my previous webinar experiences, and how can I avoid them in the future?

3. Considering the challenges outlined in the chapter, what proactive steps can I take to ensure that webinars become a valuable and seamless part of my professional development strategy?

4. Reflecting on the benefits of webinars, how can I leverage this powerful tool to not only expand my client base but also enhance my personal brand as a trusted Chartered Accountant?

5. In the context of my role as a Chartered Accountant operating in the Indian market, what additional considerations or strategies should I keep in mind when planning, organizing, or participating in webinars?

These questions can help you contemplate the chapter's content and how it applies to your specific role and goals as a practicing Chartered Accountant.

Taking Action: Your Path to Webinar Success

We divide this section into 3 parts, for leveraging webinar -as a speaker, as a participant and as an organiser.

How can you leverage webinars in any of these roles.

Speaking in Webinars:

First, let's talk about presenting in webinars. This is your opportunity to shine and establish yourself as an authority in your field.

1. Crafting Compelling Content: The foundation of a successful webinar lies in your content. Identify topics that resonate with your audience, align with your expertise, and address their pain points. Craft a clear and engaging narrative that delivers value from start to finish.

2. Mastering Presentation Skills: While it's okay to be yourself, it's essential to enhance your presentation skills. Practice speaking clearly and confidently. Pay attention to your tone, pacing, and body language. Engage with your audience as if they were right in front of you.

3. Visual Aids and Materials: Use visual aids like slides to support your content. Keep them

simple and easy to follow. Provide supplementary materials, such as handouts or guides, to help your audience delve deeper into the topic.

4. Engage with Your Audience: Encourage interaction throughout your webinar. Ask questions, conduct polls, and invite participants to share their thoughts in the chat. This fosters engagement and makes your webinar more memorable.

5. Q&A Sessions: Allocate time for Q&A sessions during and after your presentation. Addressing participant questions demonstrates your expertise and builds trust. Prepare for potential questions in advance to ensure you're ready to provide insightful responses.

Organizing Webinars:

Now, let's shift our focus to the logistics of hosting webinars. Organizing webinars effectively is crucial for a seamless and successful experience.

1. Selecting Relevant Topics: Choose webinar topics that align with your brand and cater to your target audience's needs. Research trending industry topics and gather feedback to gauge interest.

2. Webinar Planning: Create a comprehensive plan for your webinar, including objectives, target audience, date, and duration. Consider collaborating with industry experts or influencers to enhance the credibility of your webinar.

3. Promotion and Marketing: Even the best webinar needs promotion. Leverage social media, email marketing, and your professional network to spread the word. Craft compelling promotional materials that highlight the value of your webinar.

4. Testing and Technical Setup: Don't leave the technical aspects to chance. Test your equipment, software, and internet connection in advance. Familiarize yourself with the webinar platform to avoid any last-minute surprises.

1. Follow-Up and Evaluation: After the webinar, follow up with participants to thank them for attending and provide additional resources or answers to questions. Conduct post-webinar surveys to gather feedback and insights for future improvements.

2. Network – Network with each attendee and engage with them with their requirements. As an organiser you also

have the access to their email id, which with their permission can be used for knowledge sharing or further communication. Connect with each one on social media platform.

3. Social media posting – post about organising these on your SM platform. This will make you appear as an active member of the community helping you build your brand.

Attending Webinars:

As a Chartered Accountant, attending webinars is not just about learning but also about networking and staying updated with industry trends.

1. Prioritizing Webinars: Given your busy schedule, it's crucial to prioritize webinars that align with your professional development goals. Be selective and focus on high-impact webinars that offer valuable insights.

2. Active Participation: Don't be a passive observer. Engage actively by asking questions, sharing your thoughts in the chat, and participating in discussions. Networking during webinars can lead to valuable connections.

3. Note-Taking and Action Items: Take diligent notes during webinars, highlighting key takeaways and action items. After the webinar, create a plan to implement what you've learned into your practice.

1. Networking Opportunities: Leverage the opportunity to connect with speakers, fellow attendees, or industry leaders. Building a network can open doors to collaborations, partnerships, and new opportunities.

2. Asking Thoughtful Questions: When asking questions, ensure they are well-thought-out and relevant to the topic. Thoughtful questions contribute to meaningful discussions and help you stand out.

3. Social media posting – post about attending the webinar and tag the speakers, organisers and the community who organised. Share what you learnt with others. This will help you network, and share your interest in gaining knowledge too.

As you embark on this journey to embrace webinars as a powerful tool for your growth and branding as Chartered Accountants, remember that practice makes perfect. Each webinar you host or attend will provide valuable experience, helping you refine your skills and expand your professional network. Stay tuned for the upcoming sections, where we'll further explore the Indian context and share success stories specific to our field. Your commitment to continuous learning is a testament to your dedication to excellence.

Chapter 10: Tools

As a branding coach who has worked with countless Chartered Accountants, I understand the unique challenges and opportunities that you face. In this chapter, we will delve into the fascinating realm of online branding tools, specifically designed to cater to your needs in the Indian context.

Now, let's address the elephant in the room: the challenges you, as Chartered Accountants, encounter when it comes to online branding. Trust me; you're not alone in facing these hurdles. Together, we'll explore them and find effective solutions.

1. Lack of Time: As busy professionals, your time is precious. Balancing client work, audits, and compliance matters often leaves little room for online branding efforts. It's a challenge to find time to craft compelling content and maintain a consistent online presence.

Solution: We'll uncover how the right tools can help you automate tasks and save time, making online branding more manageable.

2. Complex Regulations: The financial and legal landscape in India is intricate, and navigating it online can be daunting. Ensuring that your online branding complies with relevant regulations and ethical standards is a priority.

Solution: I'll guide you on how to align your branding efforts with industry regulations while still showcasing your unique strengths.

3. Competition: The CA profession is highly competitive, with thousands of skilled professionals vying for the same clients. Standing out amidst this competition can be challenging.

Solution: We'll explore how strategic branding can help you differentiate yourself and attract the right clients.

4. Limited Awareness: Many CAs underestimate the power of online branding or simply lack awareness about the tools and strategies available.

Solution: I'll introduce you to the tools that can transform your online presence, even if you're starting from scratch.

5. Fear of Making Mistakes: The fear of making a branding blunder can paralyze your online efforts. Nobody wants to damage their professional reputation unintentionally.

Solution: We'll address this fear and learn from real-life examples to avoid common mistakes.

6. No paid marketing – CAs are not allowed to indulge in paid promotions, hence cannot use "boost post" or any such paid methods to boost their content.

By acknowledging these challenges, you're already taking the first step towards overcoming them. Throughout this chapter, we'll equip you with the knowledge and tools needed to tackle these obstacles head-on and establish a strong online presence that complements your CA practice.

So, my fellow CAs, buckle up for an exciting journey into the world of online branding. In the upcoming sections, we'll dive deeper into the common mistakes to avoid and explore the role of online branding tools in transforming your professional identity. It's time to thrive in the digital age and showcase your expertise to a wider audience. Stay tuned for more insights and practical advice!

Five Essential Tools for Online Branding

Welcome back, dear Chartered Accountants! In this section, we're diving straight into the core of our chapter: the five indispensable tools for online branding. These tools are the secret sauce to elevate your online presence and make a lasting impression on potential clients in the Indian context. Let's get started!

1. Canva: Your Creative Ally

Picture this: stunning visuals that instantly capture your audience's attention. Canva is your gateway to creating eye-catching graphics, social media posts, and marketing materials without the need for a graphic design degree. It's user-friendly, loaded with templates, and perfect for adding a professional touch to your brand. Make those festive creatives, notification posts, infographics, presentations smoothly now.

2. Social Media Posting Scheduler: Time Saver Extraordinaire

Time management is crucial for CAs. With a social media posting scheduler, you can plan and schedule your content in advance, ensuring a consistent online presence. No more rushing to post during busy work hours. These tools allow you to engage with your audience at the right times. HubSpot app and many other app offer this. You can infect schedule posts from the social media platforms too for free.

3. ChatGPT: Your Content Companion

Imagine having an AI-powered assistant that helps you generate engaging content effortlessly. ChatGPT is your writing partner, ready to craft compelling blog posts, social media captions, and even responses to client queries. It saves you time and ensures your content is on point.

4. Mail chip: for email marketing

Chartered accountants can leverage the Mailchimp app to enhance their marketing efforts effectively. Mailchimp enables them to maintain a professional online presence by creating and sending tailored email campaigns to existing clients and prospects. They can share valuable financial insights, tax updates, and industry news, positioning themselves as experts in their field. Mailchimp's analytics feature helps track campaign performance, allowing accountants to refine their strategies for better engagement. Additionally, automated workflows and personalized content ensure clients receive relevant information, fostering stronger client relationships. With Mailchimp, chartered accountants can efficiently market their services, drive client retention, and attract new business opportunities.

5. Google My Business: Local Visibility Amplifier

For CAs catering to a local client base, Google My Business is a game-changer. It ensures that your practice appears on Google Maps and local searches. Potential clients can find you easily, read reviews, and get essential information, enhancing your credibility.

6 Zoho CRM plus: Customer relations

Chartered accountants can optimize their practice using Zoho CRM Plus, a comprehensive customer relationship management solution. They can efficiently manage client relationships by organizing client data, tracking interactions, and automating appointment scheduling. The integrated Zoho Books allows seamless financial management, streamlining invoicing, expense tracking, and tax compliance. Chartered accountants can enhance customer service by promptly addressing queries and concerns through multi-channel support tools. Zoho CRM Plus also offers robust analytics, enabling accountants to gain insights into client behavior and preferences, helping them tailor services and marketing efforts effectively. This all-in-one platform empowers chartered accountants to provide top-notch financial services while efficiently managing their client base.

4. Inshot: Video editing

> Chartered accountants can utilize the InShot app to create professional video content for financial advice, tax tips, and industry updates. This user-friendly video editing tool allows them to enhance their online presence, engage clients, and share valuable insights via social media platforms, enhancing their marketing and client communication efforts.
>
> I personally use this and is very convenient

5. Zoom – you might be using Zoom only to attend some webinars or meetings. But you can use zoom to easily record your videos for social

media content. Thinking of starting that podcast but hesitant of the arrangements? Simple you need zoom, free account, start and record the podcast. The best part is your meeting is recorded in both audio and video format.

Now, let's tie it all together.

Chapter Summary

In this chapter, we embarked on a journey through the world of online branding specifically tailored for practicing Chartered Accountants in India. We started by acknowledging the challenges you face, including time constraints, complex regulations, competition, limited awareness, and the fear of making mistakes.

However, armed with the right knowledge and tools, we addressed these challenges head-on. We explored the importance of creating a robust online presence to stand out in a competitive landscape.

As your branding coach, I encourage you to explore these tools further, experiment with them, and tailor your online branding strategy to your unique strengths and aspirations. Remember, consistency is key, and your online journey is a continuous process of growth and evolution.

Stay tuned for the next sections, where we'll dive into real-life case studies, practical tips for implementation, and additional resources to further empower your online branding efforts. You're on the path to becoming a Chartered Accountant with a powerful digital presence!

Chapter 11: 3 Key Takeways

The Power of Online Presence for Chartered Accountants

In today's digital age, the importance of online presence for chartered accountants cannot be overstated. As the world's number one branding coach, I'm here to shed light on the significance of establishing a robust online presence for these financial professionals and provide you with 10 key action points to make it happen.

Why Online Presence Matters:

1. Credibility and Trust: An online presence builds credibility and trust among potential clients. When individuals can easily find you online, they are more likely to trust your expertise.

2. Global Reach: The internet knows no boundaries. With a strong online presence, you can connect with clients

from around the world, expanding your reach far beyond your local area.

3. Competitive Edge: In a competitive field like accounting, a strong online presence sets you apart from others and positions you as a leader in your industry.

4. Accessibility: Being online means clients can reach you 24/7, making it convenient for them to get in touch and seek your services.

5. Showcasing Expertise: Your website and social media profiles allow you to showcase your expertise, share valuable content, and demonstrate your knowledge in the field.

6. Networking Opportunities: Online platforms provide opportunities to connect with other professionals, which can lead to collaborations and referrals.

7. Client Education: Use your online presence to educate clients about financial matters, helping them make informed decisions.

8. Cost-Effective Marketing: Compared to traditional advertising, online marketing

is cost-effective and can yield significant returns on investment.

9. Feedback and Reviews: Online reviews and feedback from satisfied clients can bolster your reputation and attract new business.

10. Adaptation to Modern Trends: In an increasingly digital world, staying offline can make your practice seem outdated. Embracing online tools and platforms ensures you're up to date with modern trends.

10 Key Action Points:

1. Create a Professional Website: Invest in a professional website that reflects your expertise and offers valuable information to visitors. Include a biography, services offered, client testimonials, and contact information.

2. Optimize for SEO: Ensure your website is optimized for search engines (SEO). This will help your site rank higher in search results, making it easier for potential clients to find you.

3. Engage on social media: Create profiles on relevant social media platforms such

as LinkedIn, Twitter, and Facebook. Share industry insights, interact with your audience, and showcase your achievements.

4. Regularly Publish Content: Develop a content strategy that includes blogs, articles, or videos related to accounting and finance. Consistently publish high-quality content to establish yourself as an authority in your field.

5. Networking: Join online forums, groups, and communities related to accounting and finance. Participate in discussions and offer valuable insights to connect with potential clients and other professionals.

6. Email Marketing: Build an email list of clients and interested parties. Send out newsletters with valuable tips, updates, and special offers to keep your audience engaged.

7. Online Advertising: Consider using online advertising, such as Google Ads or social media ads, to target a specific audience and drive traffic to your website.

8. Client Reviews: Encourage satisfied clients to leave reviews on platforms like Google My Business and Yelp. Positive reviews can significantly impact your online reputation.

9. Professional Networking Events: Attend virtual networking events and webinars within the finance and accounting industry. This can help you establish connections and partnerships.

10. Analytics and Monitoring: Use tools like Google Analytics to track your online performance. Monitor website traffic, social media engagement, and email open rates to refine your online strategy.

In conclusion, as a chartered accountant, your online presence is your digital storefront. It's where potential clients first encounter your brand, and it's essential to make a strong impression. By following these 10 key action points, you'll not only enhance your online presence but also position yourself as a trusted and reputable financial professional in the digital world. Embrace the power of the internet, and watch your practice thrive.

Chapter 12: Offline Branding

Introduction:

In today's fast-paced digital world, it's easy to get caught up in online branding and marketing. But what many practicing Chartered Accountants often forget is that offline strategies can be just as powerful, if not more so. In this chapter, we'll delve into the world of offline branding and marketing, exploring its relevance in the digital age and how it can benefit you, the practicing Chartered Accountant.

You might be wondering, "Why should I bother with offline strategies when everything is happening online?" Well, that's a great question! Offline branding and marketing serve as the solid foundation upon which your online presence is built. It's about creating a consistent brand image that resonates with your audience, whether they encounter you at a networking event, a seminar, or through traditional media like newspapers and television.

In this chapter, we'll guide you through the intricacies of offline branding and marketing, offering insights, strategies, and actionable steps that are tailored to your needs as a Chartered Accountant. We'll explore the common mistakes to avoid, the unique challenges you face, and the thought-provoking questions that will help you craft an effective offline branding strategy.

Before we dive into the world of offline branding, it's crucial to understand the pitfalls that many professionals stumble into. By identifying these common mistakes, you can steer clear of them and set yourself on the path to success in offline branding.

1. Overlooking Consistency with Online Branding: One of the biggest mistakes is treating your online and offline personas as separate entities. Your clients and prospects should recognize your brand whether they meet you in person or online. Consistency in messaging, values, and visual identity is key.

2.   Neglecting to Define Clear Offline Objectives: Without clear objectives, your offline efforts may lack direction. Are you looking to build trust, attract new clients, or establish yourself as an industry expert? Define your objectives to tailor your offline strategies effectively.

3. Failing to Measure Offline ROI: Just like your online efforts, you should measure the return on investment (ROI) for your offline activities. This could be in terms of new clients acquired, increased brand visibility, or improved client retention. Without measurement, it's hard to know what's working and what isn't.

4. Inconsistent Brand Messaging: Your brand message should be clear, concise, and uniform across all offline channels. Inconsistencies can confuse your audience and dilute your brand's impact.

5. Ignoring the Power of Word-of-Mouth Marketing: Offline interactions often lead to word-of-mouth referrals, which can be incredibly powerful. Failing to leverage this organic marketing can be a missed opportunity.

As your dedicated branding coach, we'll guide you on how to avoid these common missteps and navigate the world of offline branding and marketing effectively. We want you to harness the full potential of offline strategies to grow your practice and establish yourself as a trusted Chartered Accountant.

In the upcoming sections, we'll address the unique challenges faced by Chartered Accountants in offline branding, provide reflective questions to help you strategize, and offer actionable steps to implement offline branding successfully in the Indian context. Stay tuned; there's a lot more valuable information to come!

Challenges Faced by Practicing Chartered Accountants

Now that we've explored the importance of offline branding and identified common mistakes to avoid, it's time to dive deeper into the unique challenges you, as practicing Chartered Accountants, might encounter on your offline branding journey.

Limited Time and Resources: As busy professionals, your time is precious. Balancing client work, compliance, and other responsibilities can leave you with little time for branding and marketing efforts. Additionally, allocating resources for offline branding might seem challenging when you're already stretched thin.

Building Trust and Credibility: Trust is the bedrock of any successful professional service. In the financial realm, where clients rely on you to safeguard their financial interests, building and maintaining trust is paramount. Offline branding plays a significant role in this, but it can be a long and demanding process.

Competition from Global Service Providers (CPA, CFA): The field of finance is increasingly global, with Chartered Accountants facing competition not only from their peers but also from global service providers like CPAs and CFAs. These international designations can be alluring to clients, making it crucial for you to stand out in the crowd.

Ethical Limitations by ICAI: The Institute of Chartered Accountants of India (ICAI) sets strict ethical guidelines for its members. While these guidelines are essential for maintaining professional integrity, they can sometimes restrict the range of marketing strategies you can employ.

Navigating the Indian Context: India's diverse cultural landscape and regional variations add another layer of complexity to offline branding. What works in one region may not work in another. Understanding and effectively navigating these regional nuances is a challenge that requires careful consideration.

As your dedicated branding coach, we understand these challenges intimately. Our goal is to equip you with the knowledge, tools, and strategies to overcome these obstacles. In the upcoming sections, we'll provide you with actionable steps and insights to address each of these challenges head-on, ensuring that your offline branding efforts are not only effective but also tailored to the unique Indian context in which you operate. Stay tuned for practical solutions that will help you excel in offline branding as a practicing Chartered Accountant.

Action Steps:

Now that we've explored the challenges and pitfalls, it's time to roll up our sleeves and get into the heart of the matter – actionable steps to supercharge your offline branding as a Chartered Accountant.

1. Crafting a Compelling Offline Brand Persona:

- ✓ Define Your Unique Branding Point (UBP): What sets you apart from other Chartered Accountants? Identify your unique strengths and qualities that make you an excellent choice for clients.
- ✓ Develop an Offline Brand Voice: Your brand voice should be consistent across all offline channels. Whether you're speaking at a seminar or networking event, your messaging

should resonate with your target audience.

- ✓ Aligning Offline Branding with Online Presence: Ensure that your offline branding efforts align seamlessly with your online presence. Your website, social media profiles, and offline materials should all reflect a unified brand image.

2. Exploring Ethical Offline Marketing Strategies:

Incorporate ICAI Guidelines: Adhering to ethical guidelines is paramount. We'll guide you on how to navigate these guidelines while still effectively promoting your services offline.

3. Leveraging Trends from Global Service Providers (CPA, CFA):

- ✓ Case Studies and Best Practices: Learn from the success stories of global service providers like CPAs and CFAs. Discover what strategies they've employed to excel in offline branding.
- ✓ Adapting Global Trends to the Indian Context: We'll help you adapt and implement these global trends within

the unique landscape of the Indian market.

4. Maximizing Word-of-Mouth Marketing:

- ✓ Provide Exceptional Service: The foundation of word-of-mouth marketing is delivering exceptional service. Happy clients become brand ambassadors, so focus on exceeding expectations.
- ✓ Encourage Referrals: Implement referral programs to incentivize satisfied clients to refer others to your services.

5. Establishing Local Networking and Partnerships:

- ✓ Identify Local Networking Opportunities: Discover local business associations, chambers of commerce, and networking events where you can connect with potential clients and partners.
- ✓ Build Trusting Relationships: Networking isn't just about collecting business cards; it's about building

genuine, trust-based relationships that can lead to valuable referrals.

As your dedicated branding coach, our mission is to provide you with actionable steps that are tailor-made for the challenges you face as a Chartered Accountant. These action steps are designed to empower you to take control of your offline branding journey.

Remember, offline branding isn't a one-size-fits-all approach. Your offline branding strategy should be a reflection of your unique strengths and values as a Chartered Accountant. By crafting a compelling offline brand persona, adhering to ethical guidelines, leveraging global trends, maximizing word-of-mouth marketing, and establishing local networks, you'll be well on your way to becoming a trusted and recognized professional in the field.

Stay tuned for the upcoming sections where we'll delve into specific strategies, reflective questions, and real-world examples to help you excel in offline branding within the Indian context. Your journey to becoming a standout Chartered Accountant in the offline world has just begun!

Inbound Marketing Strategies for Chartered Accountants:

Now that we've covered the importance of offline branding, identified common mistakes, and discussed action steps, let's delve into another critical aspect of your offline branding journey: inbound marketing strategies designed specifically for Chartered Accountants.

1. Content Creation for Offline Audiences:

✓ Create Valuable Resources: Develop informative brochures, booklets, or handouts that showcase your expertise. These materials should provide tangible value to your audience, helping them understand complex financial topics.

✓ Educational Seminars: Host seminars or workshops where you can share your knowledge with potential clients. These events not only position you as an industry expert but also offer a platform for direct interaction.

2. Utilizing Seminars and Workshops:

✓ Thought Leadership: When you present at seminars and workshops, you establish yourself as a thought leader in your field. Share insights, case studies, and practical advice that resonate with your audience.

✓ Networking Opportunities: These events aren't just about speaking; they're also excellent networking opportunities. Engage with attendees, answer their questions, and build relationships that can lead to future business.

3. Capitalizing on Public Speaking Engagements:

✓ Speaking Engagements: Whenever you have the chance to speak at conferences, industry events, or local gatherings, seize the opportunity. Public speaking enhances your visibility and credibility.

✓ Tailored Content: Customize your presentations to address the concerns and interests of your target audience. Make your content relevant and engaging.

4. Networking Events and Business Associations:

✓ Join Relevant Associations: Consider becoming a member of industry-specific associations or chambers of commerce. These affiliations can open doors to networking opportunities and referrals.

- ✓ Attend Local Events: Attend local business events, trade shows, and conferences. These gatherings are perfect for expanding your professional network.

5. Engaging in Thought Leadership:

- ✓ Publish Articles: Share your expertise by writing articles for industry publications, newspapers, or online platforms. Position yourself as a thought leader in financial matters.
- ✓ Online Platforms: Extend your thought leadership to online platforms like LinkedIn and industry forums. Engage in discussions, answer questions, and provide valuable insights.

Inbound marketing strategies are all about drawing potential clients to you through informative and valuable content. By creating valuable resources, hosting seminars and workshops, capitalizing on public speaking opportunities, engaging in networking events, and establishing yourself as a thought leader, you'll not only enhance your offline branding but also attract clients who value your expertise.

These strategies are designed to be accessible and effective, helping you connect with your target audience in a meaningful way. Stay tuned for more insights and practical tips as we continue our journey to supercharge your offline branding efforts as a Chartered Accountant.

Chapter Summary: "Offline Branding and Marketing for Practicing Chartered Accountants in the Indian Context"

In this comprehensive chapter, we explored the world of offline branding and marketing specifically tailored for practicing Chartered Accountants within the diverse landscape of India. As the world's number one branding coach for service-based businesses, our mission was to equip you with actionable insights and strategies to excel in this essential aspect of your profession.

In summary, offline branding and marketing are essential components of a successful Chartered Accountant's practice, especially within the Indian context. By avoiding common mistakes, addressing unique challenges, and implementing actionable strategies, you can create a robust offline brand presence that complements your online efforts, ultimately helping you grow your practice and become a recognized and trusted professional in your field.

Chapter 13: Public Relations

Introduction:

Hey there, practicing Chartered Accountants! Welcome to the exciting world of public relations tailored just for you. In this chapter, we'll embark on a journey to uncover the power of public relations strategies designed to elevate your professional reputation and boost your client base.

You're already well-versed in numbers and finance, but in today's world, your success isn't just about crunching digits. It's also about how you present yourself to the world, how you build trust, and how you stand out from the crowd. That's where public relations come into play.

Think of public relations as your personal brand's best friend. It's all about managing the way people perceive you and your services. In a field as competitive as Chartered Accountancy, PR can be your secret weapon.

Understanding Public Relations:

Now, let's dive deeper into what public relations really means. At its core, it's about building relationships — relationships with your clients, peers, and the wider business community.

Picture this: You're not just a CA; you're a trusted advisor, a financial guru, and a problem solver. But how will your potential clients know that? That's where PR steps in.

We'll explore how to make the most of your online presence, showcasing your expertise and creating a stellar reputation. But it's not all digital – we'll also delve into offline strategies because shaking hands and making genuine connections is still a powerful way to grow your practice.

So, get ready to learn how to shine in the world of Chartered Accountancy by mastering the art of public relations. It's all about you, your brand, and your success! Stay tuned for the next sections where we uncover common PR mistakes and delve into ethical considerations.

Action Steps:

Hello, ambitious Chartered Accountants! Now that we've explored the importance of public relations and the ethical considerations, it's time to roll up our sleeves and get into action. In this section, we'll outline actionable steps you can take to supercharge your PR efforts and propel your career to new heights.

1. Write Books and Articles for Publications: Position yourself as an authority in your field by sharing your expertise in written form. Whether it's a book, articles for financial magazines, or guest blog posts on relevant websites, becoming a published author can boost your credibility and visibility.

2. Be Invited as a Chief Guest to Events: Your knowledge is your currency, and sharing it at industry events as a chief guest can make you a sought-after figure. Attend local and national events, offer to speak, and impart your wisdom to a captivated audience.

3. Become a Speaker at Events: Take centre stage at conferences, seminars, and workshops as a speaker. Sharing your insights and experiences not only establishes you as a thought leader but also expands your professional network.

4. Organize Events: Don't wait to be invited; create your opportunities. Host workshops, webinars, or even conferences, where you're the driving force behind knowledge sharing. This not only elevates your status but also allows you to tailor events to your audience's needs.

5. Go Global: Expand your horizons by participating in international events, speaking engagements, or collaborating with global counterparts. Networking on a global scale can open doors to new opportunities and clients.

6. Measure and Adjust: Don't forget to measure the impact of your actions. Track website traffic, engagement on social media, and the growth of your professional network. If something isn't working as expected, adjust your strategy accordingly.

7. Networking: Continuously build and nurture your professional network. Attend local business chambers, industry-specific gatherings, and online forums. Networking is not just about who you know but also who knows you.

8. Continual Learning: Stay updated with industry trends and PR strategies. Enrol in courses, attend workshops, and read books to keep refining your skills.

9. Seek Feedback: Don't hesitate to ask for feedback from clients, peers, and mentors. Constructive criticism can help you fine-tune your PR approach.

Remember, it's not just about ticking off these action steps; it's about integrating them into your professional life. Each step you take should bring you closer to becoming a PR-savvy Chartered Accountant who not only excels in your field but also stands out in the crowded marketplace. Stay tuned as we explore more ways to enhance your public relations efforts!

Chapter 14: Networking for Branding

Networking is an invaluable tool for Chartered Accountants (CAs) in India seeking to amplify their professional presence and branding. In this chapter, we will delve into the art of networking specifically tailored to the needs of practicing CAs. Building a robust professional network can significantly impact your career trajectory. It's not just about who you know but how you engage with them.

As a practicing CA in India, you operate within a unique professional landscape. You understand the intricacies of Indian taxation, financial regulations, and business dynamics. However, you also face certain challenges. One significant hurdle is the limitation of not being part of business clubs like BNI. These clubs offer a platform for cross-industry networking, which can be instrumental in your branding journey. Understanding your context is the first step toward effective networking.

Networking can be a double-edged sword if not approached correctly. Many CAs fall into the trap of making common networking mistakes, such as being overly transactional or failing to follow up. These errors can hinder rather than enhance your branding efforts. In this section, we'll pinpoint these mistakes and provide guidance on how to avoid them.

To excel as a CA in India, it's crucial to acknowledge the unique challenges you face. The intricacies of our tax system, regulatory environment, and cultural nuances present hurdles that, when not addressed, can limit your professional growth. Furthermore, not participating in business clubs like BNI can mean missing out on valuable networking opportunities. Understanding these challenges is the first step toward overcoming them.

Reflective Questions for Self-Assessment

- How can I set clear networking goals to enhance my professional branding as a Chartered Accountant?

- What common networking mistakes should I avoid to ensure my networking efforts are effective?

- What are the specific challenges and opportunities of networking within the Indian context as a CA?

- How can I proactively engage in online networking platforms to expand my professional connections?

- What strategies can I employ to make the most of gender-centric clubs and associations for women CAs in India?

Action Steps for Effective Networking (500 words)

Networking is not a passive activity; it requires proactive steps to build and maintain meaningful connections. Here are actionable steps tailored to practicing Chartered Accountants (CAs) in India, aimed at boosting your networking skills and enhancing your professional branding:

1. Set Clear Networking Goals:

   ✓ Define specific objectives for your networking efforts, such as expanding your client base, collaborating with fellow professionals, or staying updated on industry trends.

- ✓ Having clear goals will help you focus your efforts and measure your networking success.

2. Leverage Offline Platforms:

- ✓ Actively engage in industry-related groups and discussions to connect with peers and potential clients.
- ✓ Attend various business events, CA events to build that strong network

3. Attend Industry Events:

- ✓ Identify seminars, workshops, and conferences related to accounting, finance, and taxation in your area.
- ✓ Attend these events to meet industry leaders, potential clients, and fellow CAs.
- ✓ Prepare a succinct elevator pitch to introduce yourself and your services effectively.

4. Local Business Associations:

- ✓ Join local business associations, such as chambers of commerce or industry-specific groups.
- ✓ Attend meetings and networking events regularly to establish yourself as a visible presence within your community.

5. Collaborate with NGOs:

   ✓ Seek opportunities to collaborate with non-governmental organizations (NGOs) on projects that align with your expertise.
   ✓ Volunteering for causes you are passionate about can lead to meaningful connections and positive brand exposure.

6. Social Clubs:

   ✓ Consider starting your own networking group or social club focused on financial professionals.
   ✓ Host regular meetings or events where professionals can exchange insights and referrals.
   ✓ If not, at least be active in attending social meetings or gatherings. Social platforms are a strong way to build network as the trust factor is high. (more on this in sales section)

7. Participate in Business Meetups:

   ✓ Look for local business meetups or networking events in your area.

✓ Actively participate in discussions and exchange contact information with potential collaborators or clients.

8. Engage in Global Forums:

   ✓ Explore online global forums and communities dedicated to finance and accounting.
   ✓ Share your expertise, ask questions, and build relationships with professionals worldwide.

9. Specialized Associations:

   ✓ Join specialized associations or organizations related to your field of expertise within accounting.
   ✓ These groups often offer exclusive networking opportunities and resources for members.

10. Consistent Follow-Up:

   ✓ After making initial connections, follow up with individuals you meet.
   ✓ Send personalized messages expressing your interest in continuing the conversation or collaboration.

11. Offer Value First:

- ✓ Approach networking with a mindset of giving before receiving.
- ✓ Share your knowledge, provide assistance, and be genuinely interested in helping others succeed.

12. Networking Calendar:

- ✓ Develop a networking calendar that outlines your networking activities throughout the year.
- ✓ Schedule regular check-ins to ensure you stay on track with your networking goals.

13. Track Your Progress:

- ✓ Keep a record of your networking efforts and their outcomes.
- ✓ Assess what strategies are most effective for you and adjust your approach accordingly.

14. Seek Mentorship:

- ✓ Consider finding a mentor who can provide guidance on effective networking.
- ✓ Learning from someone experienced can accelerate your networking success.

15. Continuous Learning:

✓ Stay updated on industry trends and best practices in networking.
✓ Invest in courses or resources that enhance your networking skills.

These action steps are designed to help you proactively build and nurture a strong network that can contribute to your professional growth and branding as a CA in India. Remember that networking is an ongoing process, and consistency is key to reaping its rewards.

As a CA, it saddens me to see drastically low number of women CA really networking. Which is why I am covering a separate section for why Networking in women centric events is essential.

The Value of Gender-Centric Clubs for Women Chartered Accountants (CAs)

Gender-centric clubs for women Chartered Accountants (CAs) play a vital role in fostering a supportive and empowering environment within a profession that has historically been male-dominated. These clubs offer numerous benefits that can significantly impact the careers and professional development of women CAs in India:

1. Networking and Peer Support:

    ✓ Gender-centric clubs provide a platform for women CAs to connect with their peers in a comfortable and understanding setting.
    ✓ Networking within these clubs allows women to exchange experiences, insights, and advice on navigating the unique challenges they may face in their profession.

2. Mentorship Opportunities:

    ✓ These clubs often facilitate mentorship programs where experienced women CAs can guide and mentor younger professionals.
    ✓ Mentorship provides valuable career advice, helps set achievable goals, and builds confidence.

3. Skill Enhancement and Learning:

    ✓ Gender-centric clubs frequently organize workshops, seminars, and training sessions tailored to the needs and interests of women CAs.
    ✓ These educational opportunities can help members enhance their technical skills, leadership abilities, and business acumen.

4. Building Confidence and Self-Esteem:

    ✓ Being part of a supportive community can boost the confidence and self-esteem of women CAs.
    ✓ Interacting with like-minded professionals who have overcome similar challenges can inspire members to reach for higher career goals.

5. Advocacy and Empowerment:

    ✓ Gender-centric clubs often engage in advocacy efforts to promote gender diversity and inclusivity within the accounting profession.
    ✓ They may work on initiatives aimed at breaking down barriers and creating equal opportunities for women in the industry.

6. Work-Life Balance:

    ✓ These clubs often address the unique work-life balance challenges that women face, especially when juggling family responsibilities.
    ✓ Members can share strategies for managing their professional and personal lives effectively.

7. Visibility and Recognition:

    ✓ Gender-centric clubs provide a platform for women CAs to showcase their expertise and accomplishments.
    ✓ This visibility can lead to increased recognition within the industry and opportunities for leadership roles.

8. Networking Beyond the Club:

    ✓ While these clubs offer a supportive community, they also encourage members to network outside the club.
    ✓ This dual approach allows women CAs to benefit from both a safe space and broader networking opportunities.

9. Inspiration for Future Generations:

    ✓ Women who are part of these clubs serve as role models for aspiring young female CAs.
    ✓ Their success stories inspire the next generation and encourage more women to pursue careers in accounting.

10. Addressing Industry Challenges:

    ✓ Gender-centric clubs can collaborate with industry organizations and regulatory bodies to address gender-related challenges.
    ✓ They may participate in discussions on policies, practices, and workplace culture to create a more inclusive profession.

11. Support During Transitions:

- ✓ Women may go through various career transitions, such as returning to work after maternity leave or pursuing new opportunities.
- ✓ These clubs offer a network that can provide guidance and support during such transitions.

12. Business Opportunities:

- ✓ Gender-centric clubs can become sources of business referrals and partnerships.
- ✓ Members often prefer collaborating with those who share their values and experiences, leading to professional opportunities.

In conclusion, networking is a powerful tool for branding and career growth, especially for practicing Chartered Accountants in India. This chapter has provided insights, strategies, and actionable steps tailored to your needs. Remember that effective networking is an ongoing process, and with dedication, it can significantly enhance your professional journey. By understanding your challenges, avoiding common mistakes, and taking proactive steps, you'll be better equipped to build a robust network that elevates your career as a CA in the Indian context.

Chapter 15: Grooming

In the competitive world of finance and accounting, the first impression often makes all the difference. As a practicing Chartered Accountant (CA) in India, you might possess unmatched expertise in numbers and finance, but have you ever considered the impact of your appearance on your clients? This chapter delves into the fascinating realm of grooming as an indispensable tool for branding, especially tailored to the Indian context.

Your grooming choices speak volumes before you even utter a word. When a client walks into your office or attends a meeting with you, they unconsciously assess your professionalism based on your appearance. For CAs, the importance of grooming cannot be overstated. It directly influences how clients perceive your competence and trustworthiness.

Imagine walking into a dentist's office, and the dentist appears dishevelled and unkempt. Your immediate reaction might be doubt about their ability, regardless of their qualifications. The same principle applies to CAs. A well-groomed appearance conveys attention to detail, discipline, and a commitment to excellence in your work.

Furthermore, grooming can significantly impact client relationships and business growth. Clients are more likely to engage with CAs who inspire confidence, and grooming plays a crucial role in building that trust. We will explore how grooming can help you stand out in the competitive CA landscape and share inspiring success stories of CAs who have witnessed remarkable transformations in their careers through effective grooming.

Understanding the significance of grooming is crucial, but equally important is avoiding common grooming mistakes that can undermine your professional image. In this section, we will identify some of the most prevalent errors made by CAs in their grooming routines.

These mistakes may range from wearing inappropriate attire to neglecting personal hygiene or overlooking the small details that matter. By learning from these mistakes and understanding their implications, you can avoid potential setbacks in your career and build a brand that resonates with clients

Reflect on these-.

- What message does your current grooming routine convey to your clients?

- Are you dressing appropriately for client meetings and professional events?

- How can your grooming choices align with your brand as a CA?

- Do your grooming habits instil confidence in your clients?

Action Steps for the Reader

Grooming is not just about looking good; it's about making a lasting impression that aligns with your professional brand as a Chartered Accountant. In this section, we will explore actionable steps that you can take to enhance your grooming practices and ensure that they resonate with your clients and peers.

1. Define Your Grooming Routine: The first step is to establish a grooming routine tailored to your profession as a CA. Consider factors like your daily schedule, client interactions, and personal style. This routine should cover skincare, haircare, attire, and personal hygiene. Consistency is key, so commit to following this routine diligently.

2. Understanding Professional Attire: Dressing appropriately for different professional situations is vital. As a CA, you may have a mix of client meetings, presentations, and office work. Invest in a versatile wardrobe that includes formal business attire, business-casual options, and traditional attire if relevant to your

practice. Ensure your attire is well-fitted, clean, and properly ironed.

3. Polishing Your Grooming Habits: Pay attention to the finer details of grooming. Maintain well-groomed facial hair, if applicable, and keep your nails clean and trimmed. Regularly visit a skilled barber or hairdresser to maintain a neat and professional hairstyle. Ensure your shoes are polished and in good condition, as they often receive more attention than you might think.

4. Align Grooming with Your Brand: Consider your personal brand as a CA. Are you aiming for a conservative and traditional image, or do you want to project a modern and innovative persona? Your grooming choices should align with your brand identity. For instance, a CA targeting tech-savvy startups might adopt a more casual yet professional appearance compared to one serving traditional industries.

5. Consult Grooming Professionals Don't hesitate to seek expert guidance. Visit a professional stylist or image consultant who can provide personalized advice on grooming and attire. They can help you understand your unique features and recommend styles that complement your image as a CA.

6. Cultural Sensitivity: In the Indian context, it's crucial to be culturally sensitive in your grooming choices. If your practice involves clients from diverse backgrounds, respect their cultural preferences and dress codes. Incorporate cultural elements into your attire when appropriate, as this can build rapport and trust.

7. Regular Self-Assessment: Grooming is not a one-time effort but an ongoing commitment. Regularly assess your grooming habits and their impact. Use reflective questions like "Am I maintaining a polished appearance?" and "Do my clients perceive me as professional and credible?" Self-awareness is the key to continuous improvement.

8. Invest in Quality: Invest in quality grooming products and attire. High-quality grooming products are not only more effective but also demonstrate your commitment to excellence. Similarly, well-made clothing lasts longer and presents a more professional image.

9. Stay Informed: Stay updated with grooming trends and best practices in the industry. Attend grooming workshops, read relevant books or articles, and follow grooming experts. Being

knowledgeable about the latest trends allows you to adapt your grooming routine to evolving standards.

10. Feedback and Adaptation Lastly, seek feedback from trusted colleagues or mentors. They can provide valuable insights into your grooming choices and their impact on your professional image. Be open to constructive criticism and be willing to adapt and refine your grooming practices based on feedback.

By following these action steps, you will not only enhance your personal grooming but also elevate your overall professional brand as a Chartered Accountant. Remember that grooming is an investment in your career and a powerful tool for building trust, credibility, and lasting client relationships in the competitive world of finance and accounting, especially in the Indian context.

While grooming primarily encompasses physical appearance, it also extends to non-verbal cues, body language, and psychological aspects that can significantly impact your branding as a Chartered Accountant (CA).

1. Body Language Matters: Effective grooming isn't limited to attire and personal hygiene. Your body language plays a crucial role in how you are perceived. Maintain good posture, make eye contact, and offer a firm handshake. These non-verbal cues convey confidence and professionalism, complementing your well-groomed appearance.

2. Psychological Impact: Grooming has a profound psychological effect, not only on how others perceive you but also on your self-confidence. When you know you look your best, you exude confidence, which is contagious and reassuring to clients. Feeling good about your appearance positively affects your overall demeanor and performance.

3. Adopting International Best Practices: The world of grooming is not static. International best practices in grooming often set the standard for professionalism. Stay informed about global grooming trends and incorporate relevant elements into your routine. This can set you apart in the Indian CA landscape and demonstrate your commitment to excellence.

4. Personal Brand Consistency: Grooming should align with your personal brand consistently. If you project a traditional image,

ensure that your grooming choices reflect that. Conversely, if your brand is more contemporary, adapt your grooming accordingly. Consistency in your personal brand across all aspects, including grooming, reinforces your professional identity.

5. Adaptive Grooming: Flexibility is key. Depending on your clientele and the nature of your CA practice, you may need to adapt your grooming. For instance, if you primarily serve conservative industries, a classic and formal grooming style may be appropriate. However, if you work with innovative startups, a more relaxed and modern approach might be better received.

6. Ongoing Self-Assessment: Self-assessment should extend beyond the basics. Reflect on the impact of your grooming choices on client interactions and business outcomes. Consider soliciting feedback from clients on whether your appearance aligns with their expectations and enhances their confidence in your services.

7. Professional Grooming Services: Consider investing in professional grooming services regularly. Visiting a skilled barber or stylist not only ensures a consistently polished look but

can also provide you with grooming advice and techniques tailored to your unique features.

Incorporating these additional insights into your grooming practices can elevate your branding as a CA in the Indian context. Remember that grooming is not a one-time effort but an ongoing commitment to excellence. It should not be seen as a superficial aspect of your professional image but as a strategic tool that reinforces your credibility, trustworthiness, and competence in the eyes of your clients and peers. By continuously refining your grooming and personal branding strategies, you can stand out and thrive in your CA career.

In this chapter, we explored the profound impact of grooming on the personal branding of Chartered Accountants (CAs) in the Indian context. Grooming goes beyond appearances; it conveys professionalism, builds trust, and influences client relationships.

Chapter 16: Tools for Offline Branding

Chartered accountants (CAs) play a crucial role in financial management, compliance, and advisory services for businesses and individuals. Effective marketing is essential for CAs to attract clients, establish their expertise, and grow their practice. Let's explore how different tools can help chartered accountants with their marketing efforts:

1. Digital Visiting cards

Haven't we all faced this, that after attending an event you collect visiting cards, and then totally forget about it. And more than often also run out of visiting cards at the events. Here comes digital visiting cards to your rescue. It enables you to save the number quickly and share all your information, "in detail" like website link, blog links, social media links, everything on the receiver's phone. Isn't this amazing?

2. Calendly :

A convenient way to organise meetings. Calendly is a free as well as paid version application. You can simply set up your events, meeting time availability and then give the link to people to block your time. This came into use during big events for me, like the GloPac where I gave this link to people so I knew whom I am meeting and at what time.

Chapter 17: Sales

As a practicing CA, your expertise in finance, taxation, and auditing is your foundation, but it's not the sole driver of your success. In today's competitive landscape, the ability to effectively sell your services is equally vital. India's dynamic business environment presents both challenges and opportunities, making it essential for CAs to not only be proficient in their field but also skilled in sales techniques.

The question arises: Why should CAs, primarily focused on technical aspects, invest their energy in sales? The answer lies in the transformative power of your knowledge. As a CA, you have the capacity to make a tangible difference in the financial well-being of individuals and organizations. Strategic sales will amplify your ability to reach those who can benefit from your expertise.

Throughout this chapter, we will dissect the core components of successful sales strategies, aligning them with your unique needs and experiences as an Indian CA. From understanding your target audience and identifying common mistakes to addressing the challenges you might face; we will equip you with practical insights and actionable steps.

We will start by exploring the significance of understanding your target audience. In a diverse nation like India, where CAs cater to a wide array of clients, recognizing the distinct needs and expectations of each segment is paramount. This knowledge will empower you to tailor your sales approach, forging deeper client relationships and fostering business growth.

In addition, we will delve into the common mistakes that CAs often make as service providers. By recognizing these stumbling blocks and learning from them, you can steer your practice toward success.

We'll also tackle the challenges inherent in the sales process. Many CAs lack formal sales training and may initially find the idea of selling services foreign or uncomfortable. The absence of a dedicated sales team, time constraints, and other hurdles can further complicate the journey. However, rest assured that we will provide you with actionable solutions to surmount these challenges.

To facilitate your personal growth, reflective questions will be interspersed throughout the chapter, encouraging you to introspect and refine your sales approach.

Furthermore, we will offer concrete action steps tailored to your needs. Whether it's developing a comprehensive sales plan, assembling a sales team, investing in sales education, or leveraging branding techniques, you'll gain the tools and insights necessary to navigate the intricate world of sales effectively.

In this chapter, our guidance won't merely be generic advice; it will be tailored to the nuances of the Indian CA landscape. We'll explore cultural and economic factors that shape sales strategies in India, underscoring the pivotal role of trust and personal connections in this dynamic market.

Our journey together promises to equip you with the knowledge, skills, and confidence to elevate your CA practice. By mastering strategic sales, you will ensure that your expertise reaches those who can benefit most from it. Let's embark on this transformative exploration of sales strategies designed exclusively for practicing Chartered Accountants in India, with the ultimate goal of propelling your CA career to new heights.

Challenges Faced by CAs in Sales

Selling financial services, even for seasoned professionals like Chartered Accountants (CAs), can be a unique and daunting endeavor. In the Indian context, where the landscape is both complex and diverse, CAs encounter a set of challenges that require careful consideration and strategic solutions. This section will explore these challenges in detail:

1. Lack of Sales Training: One of the most significant challenges for CAs is the absence of formal sales training in their education and professional development. CAs are typically trained to excel in accounting, taxation, and auditing, but they often receive little to no instruction on sales techniques. As a result, when faced with the need to sell their services, they may feel ill-equipped or uncomfortable.

Solution: We will delve into practical sales techniques and strategies tailored to the unique needs and comfort zones of CAs. This will empower them to build effective sales processes without compromising their professionalism.

2. Unfamiliarity with Sales Concepts: Many CAs may be unfamiliar with the fundamental concepts of sales and marketing. Concepts such as lead generation, lead nurturing, and conversion rates might be foreign to them. This lack of familiarity can hinder their ability to effectively attract and retain clients.

Solution: We will provide a comprehensive overview of essential sales concepts and break them down into simple, actionable steps. This will help CAs gradually build their understanding and expertise in sales.

3. Time Constraints: CAs often have demanding workloads, particularly during tax seasons and financial year-end closings. The time and effort required for sales activities can seem overwhelming, leading to neglect of crucial business development.

Solution: We will discuss time management strategies and offer tips on how CAs can integrate sales activities into their busy schedules without sacrificing the quality of their services.

4. Lack of a Dedicated Sales Team: Many small and mid-sized CA practices do not have the resources to maintain a dedicated sales team. CAs often end up juggling sales responsibilities alongside their core accounting work, which can be challenging and inefficient.

Solution: We will explore alternative approaches, such as outsourcing specific sales tasks or training existing team members to assist with sales efforts. These solutions will help CAs leverage their existing resources effectively.

5. Resistance to "Selling": The concept of "selling" financial services can be met with resistance among CAs. They may feel that promoting their expertise is at odds with their professional ethics, leading to a reluctance to engage in sales activities.

Solution: We will emphasize that selling, in the context of CA services, is about providing valuable solutions to clients and helping them achieve their financial goals. By reframing sales as a means to serve clients better, CAs can overcome this resistance and approach sales with confidence.

6. Competition: The CA profession in India is highly competitive, with a vast number of

qualified professionals. CAs may find it challenging to differentiate themselves and their services in a crowded marketplace.

Solution: We will discuss branding and marketing strategies tailored for CAs to help them stand out and establish a unique identity in the market. This will enable them to attract the right clients and thrive in a competitive landscape.

By addressing these challenges comprehensively, this section aims to equip CAs with practical insights and actionable strategies to navigate the intricacies of sales effectively. The goal is not just to help CAs sell their services but to empower them to do so in a way that aligns with their values, ethics, and the unique demands of their profession in the Indian context.

Reflect on these questions -

1. What is my current approach to sales as a Chartered Accountant, and how does it align with the strategies discussed in this chapter?

2. Do I have a clearly defined sales strategy for my CA practice, or do I rely mostly on **ad-hoc**

Chapter 18: Sales FUNNEL

Introduction :

Welcome, esteemed practicing Chartered Accountants, to a pivotal chapter in your journey to expanding your practice – "Sales Funnel." In this dynamic world of professional services, where trust and expertise are paramount, understanding the power of Sales Funnels can be a game-changer for your career.

As Chartered Accountants, you might have encountered challenges in converting potential clients into loyal ones. This challenge is compounded by the ethical limitations set by the Institute of Chartered Accountants of India (ICAI) regarding marketing and advertising. Many of you may feel hesitant to engage in paid lead generation methods, fearing a breach of these ethical guidelines.

3. client referrals and word-of-mouth marketing?

4. Am I consistently tracking and analyzing my sales performance, including metrics

like lead conversion rates and client retention rates?

5. Am I effectively leveraging digital tools and technology for lead generation, client relationship management, and marketing, or do I still rely heavily on traditional methods?

6. Do I have a team to develop my clients?

The first aspect of Understanding sales is to know your target audience –

Understanding Your Target Audience

In the world of sales for Chartered Accountants (CAs) in India, a fundamental and often underestimated key to success is a deep understanding of your target audience. Your clients, as practicing CAs, come from diverse backgrounds, industries, and financial needs. To effectively connect with and serve them, you must recognize and cater to their unique expectations. In this section, we delve into the significance of understanding your target audience and how it can elevate your sales strategies.

1. The Power of Personalization: Your clients are not uniform; they have distinct financial goals, concerns, and challenges. Understanding

their individual needs allows you to tailor your services and communication to resonate with them on a personal level. Whether you're working with small business owners seeking tax advice or corporations requiring complex auditing services, personalization fosters a stronger client-advisor relationship.

2. Navigating Diverse Industries: India is a melting pot of industries, each with its intricacies and compliance requirements. To excel in sales, you must grasp the specific challenges and opportunities faced by clients in various sectors. Whether it's the dynamic tech startup scene or the established manufacturing sector, a nuanced understanding of industry-specific issues enables you to position yourself as the go-to CA.

3. Language and Communication: India's linguistic diversity demands adaptability in your communication. Clients may prefer conducting business in regional languages or English. Understanding their language preferences and adapting your communication style accordingly demonstrates respect and professionalism.

4. Cultural Sensitivity: India's cultural diversity is unparalleled. Cultural nuances can significantly influence business interactions and decisions. A keen awareness of these nuances allows you to navigate cultural differences with grace and build stronger client relationships.

5. Financial Literacy Levels: Your target audience's financial literacy can vary widely. Some may be well-versed in financial matters, while others may need simplified explanations and guidance. Recognizing these disparities allows you to tailor your communication and educational efforts appropriately.

6. Demographic Considerations: Demographic factors such as age, gender, and location also play a role in shaping your clients' needs and preferences. For example, a young entrepreneur's financial goals may differ significantly from those of a retired professional. Understanding these demographics helps you align your services and messaging effectively.

7. Evolving Client Needs: India's economic landscape is dynamic, with changing regulatory environments and economic trends. Being attuned to these shifts enables you to anticipate

and address evolving client needs, positioning yourself as a trusted advisor.

To truly understand your target audience, consider conducting surveys, client interviews, and market research. Engage in active listening during client interactions, and seek feedback to refine your approach continually. By prioritizing a deep understanding of your clients and their diverse needs, you lay the foundation for successful sales strategies that resonate with your audience, ultimately leading to long-term client loyalty and sustainable growth in your CA practice.

Action Steps for Improving Sales, Understanding Your Target Audience, and Niche

Enhancing sales strategies for Chartered Accountants (CAs) in India involves a multifaceted approach that includes understanding your target audience and niche. In this section, we delve into comprehensive action steps that combine these elements to elevate your sales efforts and drive sustainable practice growth.

1. Develop a Comprehensive Sales Plan Tailored to Your Niche:

Start by creating a well-structured sales plan that is tailored not only to your overall business goals but also to your specific niche within the CA profession. This plan should outline your sales objectives, target audience, strategies, and tactics, all while taking into account the unique needs of your niche.

Action Step: Define your sales plan, ensuring it aligns with both your broader business goals and the specific characteristics of your niche. Identify precise sales targets and outline strategies and tactics that resonate with your niche's distinct requirements.

2. Build a Sales Team or Seek Support Aligned with Your Niche:

Within your niche, consider assembling a dedicated sales team or seeking support from professionals who understand the intricacies of your specialized field. Having a team that aligns with your niche can better address the unique concerns and opportunities your clients face.

Action Step: Evaluate your niche-specific needs and workload. Explore options for hiring sales personnel or seeking support from experts who are well-versed in your niche's nuances.

3. Invest in Niche-Specific Sales Training:

Recognizing that sales techniques may differ significantly within various niches of the CA profession, invest in sales training that is specific to your niche. Such training can provide insights and strategies tailored to the unique demands of your niche.

Action Step: Identify reputable sales training programs or resources designed explicitly for CAs operating in your niche. Dedicate time to enhancing your sales skills within the context of your specialized field.

4. Leverage Niche-Specific Branding and Marketing:

Effective branding and marketing should highlight your expertise within your niche. A strong online presence, including a niche-specific website and targeted social media outreach, can establish your authority and address the specific needs of your niche clients.

Action Step: Conduct a thorough review of your niche-specific branding and marketing efforts. Ensure that your online presence effectively communicates your niche expertise and caters to the unique requirements of your niche audience.

5. Implement Niche-Relevant Client Relationship Management (CRM):

Within your niche, clients may have specialized needs and expectations. Implement a CRM system tailored to your niche to manage and nurture client relationships effectively. This system should help you track niche-specific interactions and deliver personalized communication.

Action Step: Select and implement a niche-specific CRM system that aligns with the needs of your specialized clients. Train your team, if applicable, to use it effectively and establish niche-focused relationship management practices.

By incorporating these action steps while considering your niche and understanding your target audience, CAs can elevate their sales strategies significantly. This integrated approach ensures that your sales efforts are not only tailored to your niche but also aligned with the unique needs and preferences of your target audience. As a result, you can achieve exceptional growth and success within your specialized field in the competitive Indian market.

Summary

Enhancing sales strategies for Chartered Accountants (CAs) in India requires a strategic and tailored approach. This section outlines comprehensive action steps that encompass understanding your target audience and niche. By combining these elements, CAs can optimize their sales efforts and drive sustainable practice growth.

Key Takeaways:

- ✓ Customized Sales Plans: Develop sales plans that align with both your overall business goals and the specific characteristics of your niche within the CA profession.
- ✓ Niche-Centric Teams: Consider assembling a dedicated sales team or seeking support from professionals who understand the nuances of your specialized field to address niche-specific concerns.

- ✓ Niche-Specific Sales Training: Invest in sales training specific to your niche to gain insights and strategies tailored to its unique demands.

✓ Niche-Driven Branding and Marketing: Highlight your niche expertise through targeted online branding and marketing efforts, catering to the unique needs of your niche clients.

✓ Specialized CRM Systems: Implement niche-specific CRM systems to manage and nurture client relationships effectively, ensuring personalized communication for niche-specific interactions.

By implementing these integrated action steps, CAs can enhance their sales strategies, effectively engage with clients, and build thriving CA practices within their specialized niches. This approach ensures that sales efforts are both niche-tailored and audience-focused, ultimately leading to exceptional growth and success in the competitive Indian market.

In this chapter, we will explore how Sales Funnels can serve as a solution, aligning with ICAI's ethical framework. We'll delve into strategies that focus on education, relationship-building, and value delivery, all while maintaining the highest standards of professional ethics.

Our aim is to empower you to navigate this fine line, helping you reach your target audience effectively and ethically. By the end of this chapter, you'll not only grasp the concept of Sales Funnels but also discover practical approaches to tailor them to the unique context of the Indian CA industry. So, let's embark on this journey to transform your practice, one step at a time.

A Sales Funnel for a service-based business is a strategic framework that outlines the stages a potential client goes through before becoming a paying customer. It begins with creating awareness of your services, followed by nurturing their interest, guiding them towards a decision, and ultimately converting them into loyal clients. This funnel helps businesses systematically attract, engage, and convert leads by delivering valuable content, fostering trust, and addressing the specific needs of potential clients. It's a dynamic process designed to optimize client acquisition and retention, tailoring services to match the client's journey while delivering exceptional value and building lasting relationships.

Reflective Questions:

1. Have you ever considered how Sales Funnels can impact your practice?

2. What challenges have you faced in converting leads into clients?

3. How clear is your understanding of your target audience and their buying journey?

4. How well do you currently understand your target audience's pain points and needs, and how can you align your Sales Funnel to address these effectively?

5. What are the main obstacles or objections potential clients might have when considering your services, and how can you address these within your Sales Funnel?

6. Have you identified the key performance indicators (KPIs) to measure the effectiveness of your Sales Funnel, and

what steps can you take to continually optimize it?

7. What role does trust-building play in your Sales Funnel, and how can you enhance trustworthiness at each stage of the client journey?

8. Are you leveraging technology and automation tools effectively within your Sales Funnel, and if not, how can you incorporate them to streamline and enhance the client acquisition process?

Creating a Sales Funnel for Yourself

Examples of Sales Funnel :

Understanding practical examples of Sales Funnel stages is essential for effectively implementing this strategy in your service-based CA practice. Let's explore these stages in detail and provide examples for each:

1. Awareness Stage:

At the awareness stage, your goal is to capture the attention of potential clients and introduce them to your services without being overtly promotional. Consider the following example:

Example: Publish a series of blog posts on your website addressing common tax challenges faced by businesses. Share these posts on your social media channels and relevant online forums where business owners seek financial advice. These informative articles not only showcase your expertise but also draw potential clients into the top of your Sales Funnel. Interested readers can subscribe to your newsletter to receive more valuable insights.

2. Consideration Stage:

In the consideration stage, potential clients have shown interest and are looking for more in-depth information to evaluate your services. Here's an example:

Example: Create a downloadable resource, such as a comprehensive tax planning guide for small businesses. Promote this guide on your website, through social media, and in your email campaigns. Interested parties can access the guide by providing their contact information, allowing you to nurture these leads further.

3. Decision Stage:

At the decision stage, potential clients are evaluating whether to engage your services. Here's an example of how to guide them towards a decision:

Example: Offer a free initial consultation to businesses that have downloaded your tax planning guide. During the consultation, provide personalized insights and recommendations based on their specific financial situation. This one-on-one interaction builds trust and helps potential clients see the value you can offer.

4. Conversion Stage:

The conversion stage is where potential clients decide to become paying clients. Here's an example of how to close the deal:

Example: After the free consultation, provide a tailored proposal outlining the services you'll provide, along with transparent pricing. Offer flexible payment options and a clear path to engage your services. Ensure that the proposal emphasizes how your expertise uniquely addresses the client's needs.

5. Loyalty Stage:

The Sales Funnel doesn't end at conversion. It extends to building loyalty and retaining clients. Here's an example:

Example: After a client engages your services, continue to provide value through regular updates, informative newsletters, and proactive communication. Offer ongoing support and additional services as their needs evolve. Happy clients are more likely to refer your services to others, creating a loop where they re-enter the funnel as advocates.

These examples demonstrate how each stage of the Sales Funnel can be executed effectively in a service-based CA practice. By providing valuable content, nurturing relationships, and offering personalized solutions, you can guide potential clients through the funnel and, ultimately, foster client loyalty and growth in your practice.

Action Steps :

To successfully implement a Sales Funnel tailored for service-based businesses, especially for practicing Chartered Accountants (CAs), it's essential to break down the process into actionable steps. Here, we'll delve deeper into these steps to provide you with a comprehensive understanding of how to execute them effectively:

1. Define Your Ideal Client:

To begin, pinpoint your ideal client within the CA industry. This involves identifying specific demographics, needs, and pain points. Understand their business challenges, financial goals, and the services they are most likely to seek. By honing in on your ideal client, you can tailor your Sales Funnel content and messaging to resonate with this audience.

2. Map the Customer Journey:

Visualize the path a potential client takes from the moment they become aware of your services to when they make a decision to engage with you. This journey typically includes stages such as awareness, consideration, and decision-making. Understand what information and support clients need at each stage to progress smoothly through the funnel.

3. Create Content Strategy:

Develop a content strategy that aligns with the stages of the customer journey. For the awareness stage, consider blog posts, webinars, and informative social media content that educates potential clients about your expertise without overtly promoting your services. In the consideration stage, offer valuable resources such as eBooks, checklists, or templates in exchange for their contact information. For the decision stage, provide case studies, client testimonials, and consultation offers to build trust and encourage conversion.

4. Implement Automation:

Explore automation tools and methods to streamline and optimize your Sales Funnel. Email marketing platforms, CRM systems, and chatbots can help nurture leads and deliver personalized content. Automation not only saves time but also ensures consistency in your communication, making potential clients feel valued and supported.

5. Monitor and Adjust:

Continually track and analyze data related to your Sales Funnel's performance. Identify which stages are most effective and where potential clients might drop off. Adjust your strategies accordingly to improve conversion rates. Regularly update your content and adapt to changing client needs and industry trends.

6. Ethical Considerations:

Given the ethical limitations set by ICAI, it's crucial to ensure that your Sales Funnel practices adhere to these guidelines. Avoid any deceptive or aggressive marketing tactics. Instead, focus on providing valuable information and nurturing relationships based on trust and integrity.

By following these action steps, you'll be equipped to build and optimize a Sales Funnel tailored to the needs of practicing CAs in India. This systematic approach will help you attract, engage, and convert potential clients ethically while growing your CA practice strategically.

Chapter Summary

In the chapter "Sales Funnel," we've embarked on a transformative journey tailored for practicing Chartered Accountants (CAs) in India. The central message is clear: With strategic branding and Sales Funnel optimization, you hold the power to revolutionize your CA practice. Despite the ethical constraints set by the Institute of Chartered Accountants of India (ICAI), this chapter equips you with actionable strategies that align with professionalism and integrity.

With confidence in your abilities, you can now navigate the complex landscape of lead generation and client conversion while maintaining the highest ethical standards. The key takeaways from this chapter empower you to take charge of your practice's growth:

1. Define Your Ideal Client: Identify your target audience within the CA industry to tailor your approach effectively.

2. Map the Customer Journey: Understand the stages potential clients go through and cater to their needs at each step.

3. Create Value-Based Content: Develop content strategies that provide valuable insights and resources to attract and engage potential clients ethically.

4. Implement Automation: Utilize automation tools to streamline processes, enhance communication, and nurture leads effectively.

5. Ethical Adherence: Uphold ethical guidelines set by ICAI by focusing on trust-building, transparency, and value delivery throughout the Sales Funnel process.

In conclusion, this chapter empowers you to not only embrace the concept of Sales Funnels but to excel at its implementation. By marrying strategic branding and Sales Funnel optimization, you're poised to see remarkable growth in your CA practice while upholding the ethical standards that define your profession. Your journey towards professional success and client satisfaction begins here.

Chapter 19: Lead Generation

Introduction:

In the competitive landscape of the Indian accounting industry, practicing Chartered Accountants (CAs) face a pivotal challenge: how to consistently acquire new clients and expand their practice. This chapter, titled "Lead Generation Techniques," dives deep into the art and science of generating leads tailored to the specific needs and ethical considerations of CAs in India. As the world's foremost branding coach for service-based businesses, I recognize the paramount importance of lead generation, especially in an industry known for its trust-centric relationships.

Lead generation is not a one-size-fits-all endeavor, and for CAs, it takes on a unique dimension. The journey begins by understanding the intricate dynamics of the profession. CAs provide a service that demands precision, integrity, and expertise, and this extends to how they attract clients. This chapter serves as a guiding light for CAs, illuminating the path toward sustainable growth and client acquisition within the boundaries of ethical conduct.

Meaning of Lead Generation:

Lead generation, for CAs in India, goes beyond mere marketing; it is a strategic pursuit to identify, engage, and cultivate potential clients who require financial expertise and advisory services. In the context of this chapter, lead generation encompasses the process of initiating and nurturing relationships with individuals or businesses who could benefit from CA services.

It's crucial to recognize that lead generation for CAs differs from other industries. Clients seek CAs for their financial acumen, compliance knowledge, and business insights. Therefore, lead generation strategies must resonate with the specific needs of businesses and individuals looking for financial guidance in a complex and ever-changing regulatory environment.

This chapter will equip you, the practicing CA, with a comprehensive understanding of lead generation in the CA context. By the end, you'll be well-prepared to explore ethical and effective lead generation techniques that align with the high standards of professionalism expected in the Indian CA landscape. Whether you're a seasoned professional or just starting your practice, the insights and strategies provided here will help you navigate the intricate path of lead generation in the world of Chartered Accountancy, where trust, competence, and integrity are paramount.

Challenges Faced by CAs

Practicing Chartered Accountants (CAs) in India encounter a distinct set of challenges when it comes to lead generation and client acquisition. These challenges are not only unique to the profession but also reflect the intricacies of the Indian business landscape. As we explore the chapter on "Lead Generation Techniques," it's crucial to delve into these obstacles to understand how to overcome them effectively:

1. Ethical Limitations: CAs are bound by a stringent code of ethics, making aggressive marketing tactics or misleading promotions untenable. Balancing the need for lead generation with ethical considerations is a constant challenge. This chapter will provide insights into ethical lead generation strategies that align with the profession's integrity.

2. Competition from Big 4 Firms: Large multinational firms, often referred to as the "Big 4," dominate the Indian accounting and auditing market. Smaller CA firms struggle to compete with their extensive resources and established brand recognition. This chapter will

address how smaller firms can carve a niche and compete effectively.

3. Regulatory Hurdles: The Indian regulatory environment is intricate and subject to frequent changes. Keeping abreast of these changes and ensuring compliance while prospecting for clients can be demanding. The chapter will guide CAs on navigating the regulatory landscape to their advantage.

By understanding and addressing these challenges, CAs can refine their lead generation strategies to not only attract clients ethically but also stand out in a crowded marketplace. This chapter will provide practical solutions and insights to help CAs in India overcome these challenges and thrive in their pursuit of sustainable client growth.

Certainly, let's provide a more detailed elaboration of each action step, including one example for each, and break down each action step into three sub-steps for a comprehensive guide:

1. Collaborations and Partnerships:

Identify Synergistic Partners: Start by identifying businesses or professionals whose services align with your CA practice. For instance, if you specialize in tax consulting, consider partnering with a financial planner or an attorney specializing in estate planning.

Formalize Agreements: Once you've identified potential partners, initiate discussions to formalize collaboration agreements. These agreements should outline the terms of the partnership, such as revenue sharing, joint marketing efforts, and referral processes.

Joint Marketing and Outreach: Collaborate on marketing campaigns and outreach efforts. This can include co-hosting webinars, creating co-branded content, or jointly attending industry events. For example, if you partner with a financial planner, you could host a webinar on "Maximizing Tax Efficiency in Financial Planning."

2. Building an Online Presence:

Website Development: Create a professional website that highlights your expertise, services, and client success stories. Ensure your website is user-friendly and mobile-responsive. Incorporate a blog section where you regularly publish insightful content related to taxation, auditing, or financial planning. Make sure your website is under the code of ethics of ICAI.

Content Strategy: Develop a content strategy that addresses your target audience's pain points and questions. Publish informative articles, videos, infographics, or case studies. For instance, if you specialize in audit services, write an in-depth article about "Navigating Compliance Challenges in Auditing."

Search Engine Optimization (SEO): Optimize your website for search engines to improve visibility. Research relevant keywords and incorporate them into your content. This can be done by blogs. Google my business and being active online on platforms.

3. Leveraging LinkedIn:

Profile Optimization: Enhance your LinkedIn profile to make a strong first impression. Add a professional photo, write a compelling summary, and list your qualifications. Request endorsements and recommendations from clients or colleagues to build credibility.

Engagement Strategy: Develop a consistent engagement strategy on LinkedIn. Share industry news, insights, and thought leadership content. Comment on posts related to finance and accounting to establish yourself as an expert. For instance, share a post discussing recent tax reforms and provide your analysis.

Connection Building: Expand your network strategically by connecting with potential clients, fellow professionals, and industry influencers. Personalize your connection requests with a brief message explaining how you can add value to their network. Engage in meaningful conversations to nurture relationships.

4. Public Relations (PR):

Identify PR Opportunities: Identify opportunities to showcase your expertise in the media. This may involve monitoring industry trends and news, as well as identifying journalists or publications that cover finance and accounting topics.

Content Creation: Develop thought-provoking and informative content that can be pitched to the media. This might include opinion pieces, expert commentary on financial matters, or case studies illustrating successful financial strategies.

Media Outreach: Reach out to journalists and media outlets with your pitches. Craft compelling press releases and offer to be a source for articles related to your area of expertise. For instance, if there's a significant change in tax laws, contact a financial news outlet with your insights on its impact.

5. Sales Funnel

Top of the Funnel (Awareness): Attract potential clients through educational content and resources. Host webinars or workshops on topics like "Financial Planning for Small Businesses." Collect contact information for participants to move them to the next stage.

Middle of the Funnel (Consideration): Engage leads with personalized consultations or assessments. For example, offer a free financial audit to identify potential areas of improvement. Use this stage to understand their specific needs and pain points.

Bottom of the Funnel (Conversion): Present tailored solutions and proposals. Provide a clear path for leads to become clients, outlining the benefits of your services. Offer limited-time incentives or discounts to encourage conversion. For instance, propose a comprehensive tax planning package with a special discount for new clients.

6. Referrals –

Friends and family – these are the people who trust you the most and give you most work, but they might not exactly know what can you do expect for tax and audit. So, make them aware of the value-added services you can provide and whom are you targeting. That way they can actually connect you to right potential leads.

Clients – Let your clients know that you are open to expand. Ask them to leave review on google and if they like your work can spread a word in their network. Leads from past clients have the highest conversion rates.

Professionals – when you meet professionals, let them know your work in detail and what exactly can you bring on the table. This way they can refer work to you when they find the right lead.

These detailed action steps, exemplified by concrete examples and further broken down into sub-steps, empower the [Reader] to implement effective lead generation strategies tailored to their Chartered Accountancy practice in the Indian context.

Certainly, let's provide a more detailed elaboration of each action step, including one example for each, and break down each action step into three sub-steps for a comprehensive guide:

These detailed action steps, exemplified by concrete examples and further broken down into sub-steps, empower the [Reader] to implement effective lead generation strategies tailored to their Chartered Accountancy practice in the Indian context.

The chapter on "Lead Generation Techniques for Practicing Chartered Accountants" provides essential insights for CAs in India seeking to expand their client base. It emphasizes the importance of ethical lead generation, offering strategies to build trust while navigating unique challenges. Collaborations and partnerships are explored as a means to broaden outreach. Establishing a robust online presence and active engagement on LinkedIn are crucial in the digital age. Additionally, a well-structured sales funnel guides potential clients from awareness to conversion. This chapter equips CAs with actionable steps, fostering growth, and ensuring their practices thrive within the Indian context.

Chapter 20: Team Development

Introduction:

You must be building a great team for your firm. Starting with some partners, then some CAs under them, associates, articles, HR in some firm, and some other departments. But what about a business development or sales team?

If not what about an external support for sales?

Why are Cas in practice so hesitant in talking about sales?

They want clients but little do they ever do about sales development or having a professional help for the same.

WHY??

So, what can you do???

Incorporating a Business Development Person:

Hey there, let's talk about a game-changing strategy for your CA practice: Incorporating a Business Development Person (BDP). In our quest to grow as practicing Chartered Accountants (CAs) in the vibrant Indian market, a BDP can be your secret weapon.

Imagine having someone dedicated to spotting opportunities, nurturing client relationships, and boosting your revenue while you focus on your core skills. That's the magic of a BDP.

When you hire one, look for qualities like networking prowess, market know-how, and a results-oriented mindset. They'll be the ones weaving the threads of business growth while you provide the financial expertise.

Real stories of success will inspire you. We'll discuss practical tips for integrating a BDP into your team. With this knowledge, you can confidently make decisions that will set your practice on a path of sustainable growth, Indian style.

Building an Effective Sales Team:

1 thing we all understand, not every firm has the bandwidth to hire a sales team. So, what next?

The answer is outsourcing the lead generation activity. Is it ethical?

Let us find out

Steps you can take when you outsource sales or lead generation

1) Understanding of ethics – The main criteria while giving this work is to know if the professional understands the ethics and its importance. Just knowing the ethics is not important but understanding its relevant and why are the ethics in place is as crucial, only then will the professional work with full integrity. So, find a professional, say a CA only.

2) Given results – Find the results generated before. What was the leads generated, conversions that happened and if they have any references.

3) ROI – look at the ROI and if it fits your pocket

Outsourcing lead generation is ethical, till the steps taken are within the premises of the ethical code.

Chapter 21

Leveraging ICAI for Practicing Chartered Accountants in India

In this comprehensive chapter, we will delve into the myriad opportunities and resources provided by the Institute of Chartered Accountants of India (ICAI) and how practicing Chartered Accountants (CAs) in India can strategically leverage them. As the world's number one branding coach for service-based businesses, my mission is to guide you through the process of benefiting from ICAI, growing your professional network, generating leads, and effectively marketing yourself within the Indian context.

Importance of ICAI for a Practicing CA

ICAI stands as the bedrock of the accounting profession in India, offering a multitude of benefits to its members. One of the foremost advantages is the trust and credibility it imparts. Being an ICAI member adds a significant layer of trustworthiness to your professional image, a vital factor in attracting and retaining clients. For instance, consider the case of CA Alok, who, after obtaining ICAI membership, found that prospective clients were more inclined to trust his financial advice, leading to a substantial increase in his client base.

Furthermore, ICAI continually updates its members with the latest developments in accounting, taxation, and finance through a variety of channels. This not only keeps you informed but also enhances your knowledge and skills, making you a more valuable asset to your clients.

Networking Events Organized by ICAI

ICAI conducts an array of networking events, ranging from local branch meetings to national conferences, all of which serve as fertile grounds for expanding your professional circle. Let's take the example of CA Priya, who actively participated in her local ICAI branch meetings. Over time, she cultivated valuable connections with fellow CAs and industry experts. These connections not only led to collaborations on complex projects but also opened doors to new clientele.

Attending these gatherings also exposes you to fresh ideas, trends, and industry insights. By engaging in meaningful conversations and sharing your expertise, you can position yourself as a go-to professional in your field, further enhancing your credibility.

Networking Firms and Committees in ICAI

ICAI encompasses various committees and local chapters, each offering unique networking opportunities. By actively engaging with these committees and chapters, you can dramatically expand your professional connections. For instance, CA Rajesh joined the Taxation Committee of his local ICAI chapter. Through his involvement, he not only gained access to a vast network of tax professionals but also collaborated with them on tax-related workshops and seminars.

Moreover, these platforms provide you with the chance to work on projects and initiatives that can boost your visibility and expertise. CA Sneha, for example, became part of the Sustainability Committee and co-authored a research paper on sustainable accounting practices. This accomplishment significantly enhanced her professional reputation and attracted environmentally conscious clients.

Certifications for Members

ICAI offers an impressive array of certifications and courses tailored to the needs of CAs in various specializations. Pursuing these certifications can elevate your skillset and make you a sought-after professional. Consider CA Ramesh, who completed the Certified Information Systems Auditor (CISA) certification offered by ICAI. This specialized qualification not only deepened his knowledge but also enabled him to offer specialized services to clients seeking cybersecurity expertise.

These certifications not only enhance your competence but also set you apart in the competitive CA landscape. They are badges of expertise and can be showcased to potential clients as a testament to your commitment to continuous professional development.

Publications by ICAI

ICAI consistently publishes journals, research papers, newsletters, and magazines that keep CAs updated on industry trends, regulations, and best practices. Contributing articles or research papers to these publications can establish you as an industry thought leader and attract clients who value your expertise. For instance, CA Deepak authored an article on the impact of the Goods and Services Tax (GST) in an ICAI journal. This publication not only positioned him as a GST expert but also led to numerous inquiries from businesses seeking GST advisory services.

To leverage ICAI publications effectively, you can follow these steps:

1. Identify your area of expertise within the CA domain.

2. Keep an eye on trending topics and emerging issues.

3. Conduct thorough research and analysis.

4. Draft a well-researched article or research paper.

5. Submit your work to the relevant ICAI publication.

By following these steps and contributing valuable content to ICAI publications, you can establish yourself as a thought leader and attract clients who seek your specialized knowledge.

Speaking at Events and Organizing Study Circles

Becoming a speaker at ICAI events or organizing study circles can be a powerful way to enhance your reputation and expand your network. When you share your expertise as a speaker, you position yourself as an authority in your field. For example, CA Shreya was invited to speak at an ICAI seminar on tax planning strategies for small businesses. Her informative and engaging presentation not only earned her accolades from attendees but also led to several new client inquiries seeking her tax expertise.

Similarly, organizing study circles within your local ICAI chapter can provide a platform for knowledge exchange and networking. CA Karan initiated a study circle focused on emerging accounting technologies. This initiative not only allowed him to share his knowledge but also attracted CAs interested in staying updated on technology trends. These study circle participants later became valuable contacts in his professional network.

Organizing Events with ICAI

Collaborating with ICAI to organize events can showcase your leadership skills and broaden your reach. CA Nandini partnered with her local ICAI chapter to organize a financial literacy workshop for small business owners. This event not only benefited the local community but also positioned her as a socially responsible CA. It garnered positive media attention and led to numerous inquiries from entrepreneurs seeking her financial advisory services.

To organize events with ICAI, you can follow these steps:

1. Identify a relevant topic or theme that aligns with the interests of your target audience.

2. Propose the event idea to your local ICAI chapter or committee.

3. Collaborate on planning and execution, ensuring it meets the needs of CAs and the broader community.

4. Promote the event through various channels to attract attendees.

By becoming a speaker at events and actively participating in event organization, you not only contribute to the professional development of your peers but also position yourself as a prominent figure in the CA community, leading to increased opportunities for networking and business growth.

Action Steps

To leverage ICAI effectively and maximize its benefits, consider the following comprehensive action steps:

1. Membership Engagement: Become an active member of your local ICAI chapter and committees. Attend meetings, seminars, and workshops regularly to network and stay updated.

2. Certification Pursuit: Identify certifications or courses that align with your career goals and areas of interest. Enrol in these programs to enhance your expertise.

3. Networking Initiatives: Actively engage with fellow CAs, industry experts, and potential

clients at ICAI networking events. Collaborate on projects and initiatives to expand your professional circle.

4. Publication Contributions: Research and write articles or research papers for ICAI publications. Share your knowledge and insights to position yourself as an industry authority.

5. Speaking Engagements: Seek opportunities to speak at ICAI events and share your

In conclusion, by taking proactive action steps, including membership engagement, certification pursuit, networking initiatives, publication contributions, speaking engagements, and event organization, CAs can fully leverage ICAI's resources to achieve professional growth and success in the dynamic world of Chartered Accountancy within the Indian context.

Chapter 22: Hiring a Branding Strategist

We covered so many strategies in the book, from building your brand strategy, to online branding and offline branding, understanding how to get leads, convert into sales, and how can you leverage ICAI to grow.

Some CA's who are passionate and enthusiastic might end up walking the path and achieving the results.

But what about the some who aspire to grow, but either do not have the time, band width or team to really indulge in these extensive steps?

There are challenges that Cas face when they ride the branding journey.

Let's dive into the challenges that practicing Chartered Accountants (CAs) often encounter in their branding journey. As your trusted branding coach, I'm here to shed light on these hurdles and, more importantly, how to overcome them.

Limited Knowledge of Branding Strategies:

Many CAs are experts in finance and accounting, but when it comes to branding, they might feel like they're in uncharted territory. Branding involves creating a distinct image and message for your practice, which may not be part of your traditional skill set. The challenge here is to bridge this knowledge gap and learn how branding can elevate your CA practice.

Balancing Branding with a Busy Team:

You're not just a solo player; you have a team to manage. Ensuring that everyone on your team aligns with your brand can be tricky. The challenge lies in finding the time and resources to train and educate your team about your brand's values, messaging, and vision while managing day-to-day operations efficiently.

Ethical Limitations in Marketing:

Ethics are at the core of the CA profession, and rightly so. But this can pose a challenge when it comes to marketing and branding. You must navigate these ethical boundaries carefully. It's essential to learn how to promote your services effectively while maintaining the highest standards of integrity and professionalism.

Competition from Big 4 Firms:

The presence of giant firms can be intimidating. You might wonder how to stand out in a market dominated by these industry giants. The challenge here is to differentiate yourself and demonstrate your unique value to clients. It's not about competing head-to-head but carving your niche.

Addressing these challenges starts with education and a willingness to adapt. As your branding coach, I'll provide you with strategies and insights tailored to your needs as a CA. In the upcoming sections, we'll delve deeper into each challenge, offering practical solutions and real-life examples from successful CAs who have overcome these hurdles. Remember, every challenge is an opportunity to grow and strengthen your brand. So, let's tackle them together and pave the way for a more impactful CA practice.

Absolutely, let's explore the paramount importance of seeking professional support in your branding journey as a practicing Chartered Accountant (CA).

Accelerating Your Branding Journey:

First and foremost, professional support acts as a turbo boost for your branding efforts. You're a CA, a specialist in financial matters, and your time is precious. With professional guidance, you can skip the trial-and-error phase and swiftly develop a powerful brand presence in less time.

Avoiding Costly Mistakes:

Branding can be a complex terrain, and making errors can be expensive, not just in terms of money but also in terms of your brand's reputation. Professional support provides you with a roadmap to avoid these costly mistakes, ensuring your brand remains untarnished.

Accessing Specialized Knowledge:

Branding experts bring a wealth of knowledge and expertise to the table. They're well-versed in the intricacies of creating and sustaining a brand in the competitive market. Their insights and strategies are tailored to your unique needs as a CA, ensuring that your brand is both compelling and authentic.

Guidance in Ethical Branding:

As a CA, ethical considerations are paramount. Professional support helps you navigate the fine line between effective branding and maintaining your professional ethics. You'll learn how to market your services ethically while upholding the integrity of your profession.

Staying Ahead of the Big Players:

In the competitive world of Chartered Accountancy, it's not just about surviving; it's about thriving. Big 4 firms and other giants are your competitors, but with professional support, you can learn how to carve your niche, stand out, and attract your ideal clients.

Time and Resource Optimization:

Your time is valuable, and juggling branding efforts with your CA practice can be overwhelming. Professional support streamlines your branding process, making it efficient and allowing you to focus on what you do best - serving your clients.

Accelerated Growth: By harnessing their expertise, you fast-track your brand's growth. You'll see results sooner, attracting more clients and opportunities. This acceleration propels you ahead of the competition.

Staying on the Cutting Edge: The branding landscape is ever-evolving. Professionals stay updated on the latest trends, tools, and strategies. Their guidance ensures your brand remains relevant and competitive in a rapidly changing market.

Confidence in Branding: When you have experts by your side, your confidence in branding soars. You'll be better equipped to communicate your brand's value to clients, creating trust and loyalty.

Choosing the Right Professional Support

Selecting the right professional support for your branding journey as a practicing Chartered Accountant (CA) is a critical decision that can greatly influence the success of your brand. Here, we'll explore the key factors to consider when making this important choice.

1. Industry Expertise:

Ensure that the professional support you choose has a deep understanding of the CA profession and the intricacies of the financial industry. Look for experts who have a track record of working with CAs and service-based businesses. Their industry-specific knowledge is invaluable.

2. Ethical Acumen:

As a CA, ethics are the cornerstone of your profession. It's vital that the professional support you engage with comprehends the ethical issues and constraints faced by CAs in branding and marketing. They should be adept at crafting branding strategies that align with the highest standards of integrity and professionalism.

3. Track Record and Portfolio:

Review the past work and success stories of the professionals or agencies you're considering. Look for evidence of their ability to deliver results in terms of brand development and growth. Testimonials and case studies can provide insights into their capabilities.

4. Compatibility and Communication:

Effective collaboration is key. Ensure that there is good chemistry and communication between you and the professional support team. You should feel comfortable discussing your brand vision and goals openly.

5. Tailored Approach:

Each CA practice is unique, and a one-size-fits-all approach may not be suitable. Seek professionals who are willing to tailor their strategies to your specific needs, considering your practice's strengths, weaknesses, and goals.

6. Budget Considerations:

Understand the financial aspects of the partnership. Be transparent about your budget, and make sure the professional support's fees align with your financial resources. It's crucial to strike a balance between quality and affordability.

7. Long-term Commitment:

Branding is not a one-time endeavor; it's an ongoing process. Choose professionals who are committed to long-term success and are willing to adapt their strategies as your CA practice evolves.

8. References and Recommendations:

Don't hesitate to ask for references from their previous clients and seek recommendations from colleagues in your industry. Hearing about others' experiences can provide valuable insights.

By carefully evaluating these factors, you can make an informed decision when choosing professional support for your branding efforts. Remember, the right support can empower you to navigate the challenges and maximize the benefits of branding while upholding the ethical standards expected of a Chartered Accountant.

In this chapter, we embarked on a transformative journey for practicing Chartered Accountants (CAs) into the world of branding, guided by the professionals like us.

In essence, this chapter served as a comprehensive guide for CAs, providing them with the knowledge and tools to harness professional support and elevate their brand identity, ultimately leading to enhanced success in the competitive world of Chartered Accountancy. It's a journey of transformation and growth, and the possibilities for CAs in the realm of branding are truly boundless.

So, embrace the idea of professional support as your secret weapon in building a powerful brand identity. Together, we'll unlock the full potential of your CA practice.

CONCLUSION -

Throughout this book, we have delved into the nuances of branding strategies tailored specifically for CAs. From ethical considerations to innovative online and offline approaches, the insights provided aim to empower you to build a brand that resonates with integrity, professionalism, and value. Now, as we conclude, let us reflect on the transformative potential of embracing branding and why it is no longer a choice but a necessity for CAs aiming to thrive in the modern era.

The Need for Branding in the Modern Era

In today's interconnected and digitally-driven landscape, branding is not just about logos or slogans; it is about creating a lasting impression that aligns with your core values and expertise. For Chartered Accountants, branding represents an opportunity to:

Differentiate Yourself: The marketplace is saturated with professionals offering similar services. A strong brand helps you stand out by highlighting your unique value proposition, whether it is niche expertise, exceptional client service, or innovative solutions.

Build Trust and Credibility: A consistent and professional brand conveys reliability and authority, two qualities essential for a CA. Clients are more likely to engage with professionals who project a credible and trustworthy image.

Attract the Right Clients: Branding allows you to target your ideal clients effectively. Whether you specialize in startups, SMEs, or multinational corporations, a well-crafted brand ensures you attract clients aligned with your expertise and goals.

Future-Proof Your Practice: In an age where digital transformation is reshaping industries, branding equips you with the tools to stay relevant and adaptable, ensuring long-term success.

Ethical Branding: The Foundation of Success

As CAs, you operate in a profession governed by strict ethical standards. It is imperative that your branding efforts reflect these principles. Ethical branding ensures that your marketing strategies uphold the values of transparency, honesty, and respect for professional boundaries.

Avoid Over-Promising: Your brand should set realistic expectations. Overstating your capabilities can lead to client dissatisfaction and harm your reputation.

Maintain Confidentiality: In all your branding efforts, be cautious not to disclose sensitive client information, even inadvertently.

Adhere to Professional Guidelines: Familiarize yourself with the regulations surrounding advertising and marketing for CAs in your jurisdiction to ensure compliance.

By prioritizing ethics in your branding journey, you build a reputation that not only attracts clients but also fosters long-term relationships based on trust and mutual respect.

Leveraging Online Strategies

The digital revolution has opened up a world of opportunities for CAs to connect with clients and showcase their expertise. Some key takeaways from our exploration of online branding include:

Website Development: A professional website serves as your digital storefront. Ensure it is user-friendly, informative, and optimized for search engines to increase visibility.

Social Media Presence: Platforms like LinkedIn are invaluable for CAs to share insights, network with peers, and engage with potential clients. Regularly posting thought leadership content positions you as an expert in your field.

Content Marketing: Blogging, webinars, and e-books allow you to share valuable knowledge while subtly promoting your services. High-quality content demonstrates your expertise and builds credibility.

Online Reviews and Testimonials: Encourage satisfied clients to leave positive reviews online. Testimonials act as powerful endorsements that influence prospective clients.

Offline Strategies: The Power of Personal Connections

While online strategies dominate in the digital age, offline branding remains equally significant. Face-to-face interactions and traditional marketing approaches foster personal connections that technology cannot replicate. Key offline strategies include:

Networking Events: Attend industry conferences, seminars, and local business events to build relationships and expand your professional network.

Workshops and Seminars: Hosting educational sessions not only showcases your expertise but also positions you as a thought leader in your community.

Community Involvement: Participating in local initiatives or offering pro bono services enhances your visibility and strengthens your reputation as a socially responsible professional.

Print Media: Brochures, business cards, and professionally designed stationery continue to be effective tools for branding in the offline world.

Overcoming Common Challenges

Building a brand comes with its challenges, especially for professionals who are new to marketing. Common concerns include time constraints, lack of expertise, and fear of overstepping ethical boundaries. However, these challenges can be addressed by:

Starting Small: Focus on one or two branding strategies initially, such as improving your LinkedIn presence or attending local networking events.

Seeking Professional Help: Collaborate with branding consultants or digital marketing experts who understand the unique requirements of CAs.

Continuous Learning: Stay updated on branding trends and best practices to refine your approach over time.

The Rewards of Branding

The effort you invest in building your brand will yield substantial rewards. A strong brand leads to increased visibility, better client retention, and enhanced professional satisfaction. It also opens doors to new opportunities, such as speaking engagements, collaborations, and leadership roles within your industry.

Moreover, branding contributes to personal growth. As you define and communicate your values, strengths, and vision, you gain a deeper understanding of your own professional identity. This clarity empowers you to set meaningful goals and achieve greater fulfilment in your career.

A Call to Action

As we conclude this book, the message is clear: Branding is not a luxury; it is a necessity for Chartered Accountants who aspire to thrive in today's competitive landscape. Embrace the principles, strategies, and insights shared in these pages to create a brand that reflects your unique expertise and values.

Remember, branding is a journey, not a destination. It requires consistent effort, adaptability, and a commitment to excellence. But the rewards—both tangible and intangible—are well worth the investment.

Take the first step today. Reflect on what sets you apart as a CA and how you want to be perceived by clients and peers. Then, start crafting your brand—one that embodies your professionalism, expertise, and vision for the future.

The world needs trusted advisors who not only deliver exceptional services but also inspire confidence and trust. By embracing branding, you position yourself as a leader in your field, ready to make a lasting impact on the lives and businesses you serve.

Your journey to success begins now. Go ahead, and let your brand speak for you.

About us -Portraiture

We are a team of professionals working towards spreading the message that Personal Branding, for individuals, professionals and entrepreneurs is as important as the branding of a company.

Let me ask you, are you ready to make an impact with a strong Personal Brand?

If the answer is YES, connect with us now

At Portraiture, we firmly believe that everyone has immense potential waiting to be unleashed. It's a matter of tapping into our strengths, discovering our true selves, and presenting our best version to the world. We understand that each client is unique, and we work closely with them to deliver customized solutions that set them apart from the rest.

Our team comprises of highly motivated professionals who collaborate with talented content writers to ensure that every project is a success.

About The Author

CA Parinita Adukia is a dynamic and visionary professional with a diverse career that spans across finance, consulting, and branding. With six years of experience in the finance sector, she transitioned to explore new opportunities in 2015 and founded **Portraiture**, a venture dedicated to making a meaningful impact in the world of personal branding and professional growth.

As the Strategy Head and Chief Consultant at Portraiture, Parinita has spearheaded numerous branding projects, offering strategic guidance and consultancy to clients from some of the most esteemed organizations globally, including **PwC, Ernst & Young (EnY), BDO, TCS, Maersk, HSBC, HDFC, Kotak**, and many others. With a deep understanding of branding and positioning, Parinita has been instrumental in elevating the professional image of numerous clients, including **UpGrad, Kotak Bank, Times of India, LIC, Arcon Technologies, PwC, ICAI, NMIMS, Decimal Point Analytics**, and more.

A passionate advocate for personal and professional development, Parinita has coached over **25,000 Chartered Accountants (CAs)** on crucial skills such as **presentation, personal branding, etiquette, and professional grooming**. Her mission is to reshape the perception of CAs, transforming them into **dynamic, intellectual change-makers** who are integral to driving economic growth.

With her unique vision, Parinita is committed to leaving a lasting positive impact on the CA community, ensuring that their "BRANDING" reflects their true potential and influence in the modern professional world.

Connect with us -

portraiturepari@gmail.com

www.portraiturebypari.com

Our podcast links -

https://youtu.be/Ye1lgFjb2Jk

https://open.spotify.com/show/0JuARvbI8BQQkK
BxIz6l5F?si=4tSZXiHES_ag3bjaUDj2OA%0A

Our social media links -

Instagram
- https://www.instagram.com/portraiture_brandin
g?igsh=MTE0bGZpMDR5ZTR6dQ==

LinkedIn-

https://www.linkedin.com/company/portraitureby
pari/